Becoming a Makeover Congregation

A Story of Hope, Renewal, and Possibility

Beth A. Olson

CSS Publishing Company, Inc.
Lima, Ohio

BECOMING A MAKEOVER CONGREGATION

FIRST EDITION
Copyright © 2019
by CSS Publishing Co., Inc.

Published by CSS Publishing Company, Inc., Lima, Ohio 45807. All rights reserved. No part of this publication may be reproduced in any manner whatsoever without the prior permission of the publisher, except in the case of brief quotations embodied in critical articles and reviews. Inquiries should be addressed to: CSS Publishing Company, Inc., Permissions Department, 5450 N. Dixie Highway, Lima, Ohio 45807.

Library of Congress Cataloging-in-Publication Data

Names: Olson, Beth A., author. Title: Becoming a makeover congregation : a story of hope, renewal, and possibility / Beth A. Olson. Description: First edition. | Lima, Ohio : CSS Publishing Company, Inc., [2019] Identifiers: LCCN 2018058910| ISBN 9780788028137 (pbk.) | ISBN 0788028138 (pbk.) | ISBN 9780788028144 (ebk.) | ISBN 0788028146 (ebk.) Subjects: LCSH: Messiah Lutheran Church (Janesville, Iowa) | Evangelical Lutheran Church in America. Northeastern Iowa Synod. | Church renewal--Lutheran Church. | Lutheran Church--Ohio. | Small churches--Iowa. Classification: LCC BX8076.J36 O57 2019 | DDC 284.1/77734--dc23

For more information about CSS Publishing Company resources, visit our website at www.csspub.com, email us at csr@csspub.com, or call (800) 241-4056.

e-book:
ISBN-13: 978-0-7880-2814-4
ISBN-10: 0-7880-2814-6

ISBN-13: 978-0-7880-2813-7
ISBN-10: 0-7880-2813-8   PRINTED IN USA

To Bob, for his constancy of belief,
and
to Ariana, for her encouragement and good humor.
With love and gratitude.

Acknowledgments

I am deeply appreciative of my family's support and sustenance during the lengthy course of bringing this book to life. Their love, laughter, and encouragement are gifts they opened and shared with blessed regularity. Thankfully, they continue to do so, too!

Numerous others have contributed to this book finally becoming a reality, and I am thankful to them, also: Family members, teachers and friends over the decades who have supported and encouraged me to write--and to keep writing.

Those who have so graciously called me to serve as their pastor:

Everyone associated with Messiah Lutheran Church, where the bulk of this story is set, especially those who believed transformation was possible and who acted on that belief in ways that continue to inspire and encourage.

Also, the people of St. John, Nashua; First, Decorah; St. James, Allison; American, Grundy Center; St. Paul's and Redeemer, Waverly; all Lutheran and all in Iowa;

The congregation that started me on the road to ministry, Little Elk Creek Lutheran, Menomonie, Wisconsin;

The congregation at St. Timothy, Hudson, that so generously shares ministry together;

Early readers who gave helpful feedback and have been waiting patiently to see this book come together:
Pastor Dennis Dickman and Dr. Ron Matthias for their enthusiasm and belief that this is a story that needs to be told.

Later readers who haven't been waiting quite as long and who further refined and polished this story through their comments, questions, and stylistic advice: Michelle Byers, Andrea Sherwood, Jo and Hank Bagelmann, Sally Malcolm.

Bishop Steven Ullestad for his kind and thoughtful introduction, and the staff at the Northeastern Iowa Synod for their support, laughter and coffee breaks, and for the numerous ways they work as a team to make transformation a possibility for many.

- The prayer team at American Lutheran Church, Grundy Center, Iowa, whose persistence in prayer I am grateful for.
- The various congregations in Northeastern Iowa who have invited me to be their supply preacher over the years, especially when I was on leave. What fun it was to be in so many places and to see so many slices of ministry. Thank you for your ideas and your welcome!
- Rochelle Melander, The *WriteNow!* Coach, for bringing her professional sensibilities and suggestions to the structure and details of this book.
- Karen Thalacker and Rachel Riensche for their advice in matters legal for this first-time book author.
- Jo Riker, for her wisdom and encouragement.
- Michael Sherer for his critique, feedback, and gentle push along the way that helped keep this project moving forward.
- Matt Sallee of Waterloo Industries for the toolbox picture that I used as a visual reference when writing The Makeover Tool Chest section.
- Pastor Jenna Couch for the conversations about social media usage.
- Friends and colleagues too numerous to list who cheered on the transformation at Janesville and this book's development including, but not limited to, William Hamm, Charles Lutz, Harold and Grace Kurtz, and Jim Gardner.
- Pastor Joelle Colville-Hanson for her special attention to the "Media Today" section and for pointing me to Meredith Gould's helpful resource, *The Social Media Gospel*.
- All those at CSS: Missy Cotrell, George Reed, Sue Sonntag, Rebecca Allen, Karyl Corson, David Runk and other staff unknown to the author.

The author extends her apology for any mistakes or omissions. They are unintentional and reflect more than anything else the numerous starts and stops over the past years of getting this story told.

Table of Contents

Introduction	9
Chapter 1: The Oldest City in Bremer County	11
Chapter 2: Iowa Skepticism Meets Iowa Determination	15
Chapter 3: From Snowforts to Glowsticks	21
Chapter 4: Worship, Welcome, and a Relaxed Fit	27
Chapter 5: The Body of Christ, Living Care Packages	35
Chapter 6: Communicating Clearly	43
Chapter 7: Outside the Comfort Zones: Stewardship and Other Lessons	49
Chapter 8: The Song Is Right, but There's More to it Than That	61
Chapter 9: Looking to the Future	67
Chapter 10: Leaving Well	71
Chapter 11: The Makeover Tool Chest	75
Drawer 1: Get the Facts	76
Drawer 2: Keep Moving	77
Drawer 3: Welcome Children	79
Drawer 4: Pay Attention	81
Drawer 5: Share the Ministry	83
Drawer 6: Communicate Clearly	85
Drawer 7: Learn Your Lessons	87
Drawer 8: Mine Your Assets	88
Drawers 9 and 10: Looking to the Future and Leaving Well	92
For Clergy	94
Afterword	95
About the Author	96

Introduction

Pastor Olson shares the story of one of the congregations that she has led into a time of transformation as a model for renewal of ministry and mission. Messiah's history included ministry during difficult and sometimes tragic times and remarkable economic crises in the area. Pastor Olson brought a message of hope and a pathway through the anxiety and depression.

Weaving practical concepts and theologically sound messages of servanthood, this treatise offers an avenue for renewal in congregations facing challenging circumstances. It is a book to be celebrated by rolling up one's collective sleeves and doing God's work with our hands.

The Rev. Dr. Steven L. Ullestad
Bishop, Northeastern Iowa Synod,
Evangelical Lutheran Church in America

Chapter 1

The Oldest City in Bremer County

"I've just got to come to church because I never know what might happen!"
— Erwin Kuker

Nestled near the gently meandering Cedar River and bordered by the Avenue of the Saints lies the bedroom community of Janesville, Iowa, population roughly 1,000. The town celebrated its sesquicentennial in 1999. It's a pleasant community with friendly people who possess the kind of civic pride common in some smaller towns. Businesses include a lumberyard, a steakhouse, a bar, a bank branch office, a family welding business, and a few others. Citizens seem to like things the way they are. The town still has its own K-12 school of which the townspeople are fiercely proud. Even though there are school sharing arrangements with Waverly (five miles to the north) for academics, the school maintains its independence and recently built an addition.

One new housing development sprang up a few years ago on the west edge side of town, and now there's another area under development on the east. This, despite the fact that more than one street in Janesville was designed to dead-end. For those looking for the quiet pace of small town life, Janesville fits the bill for many. The amenities of larger cities are accessed by driving to Waverly (population roughly 10,000) or by driving to the Cedar Falls-Waterloo area (combined population roughly 105,000). Both areas have colleges and recreation venues that enhance the quality of life for residents of the Cedar Valley, so-named because of the Cedar River that flows through the towns.

Getting Started

In the 1950s, several Janesville families came together and decided they wanted to have a church in their hometown instead of driving elsewhere for worship. The momentum caught on and in the mid-50s, the fledgling congregation dedicated its small building. Never intending that the 30x60 structure with eight-foot ceilings be the permanent church, the congregation nevertheless met in that facility for 43 years.

Picture that house: Ranch style, roughly average-size, but with no room divisions — just one large, open space that serves as a sanctuary. The ceiling is low and flat. The windows are plain, old-fashioned, and double hung. The carpet is nondescript. The building sits quietly on a tree-lined street.

On a Sunday morning thirty to forty people, mostly older adults, are gathered for worship, accompanied by an aging electronic organ. Few children can be seen or heard. The basement is damp and smells of mold, except during coffee fellowship hour, when coffee and tasty treats are plentiful and fragrant.

The building itself was never supposed to be the actual church for long. The young congregation, started in 1956, planned to eventually build a "real church" and turn the present building into a parsonage. The structure was currently aging and leaking and members had more doubts than hopes.

This was Messiah Lutheran Church when I accepted the call to be its pastor in 1996. The church council and call committee made it clear from the start: it was time to build a church. My husband and I said we'd give it three years. If nothing started to move by then, well....

Nine and a half years later, I moved on, but the experience left me thinking that some day I must tell the story of this makeover congregation that came to life through love, hard work, God's grace, and a willingness to dare. All over the country similar stories are evolving — some with hope, some with despair — and pastors and parishioners are looking for ideas and solutions. Can small rural congregations survive? Can they do more than survive? This book tells the story of how one congregation did just that. Along with the ideas and strategies contained in this resource is hope for those parishes willing to dare, to risk, to dream — and to trust God.

Telling the Story

Part of why I wrote this book was to share the treasures of this particular pastoral journey. Not only was the congregation transformed, so was I. I'd had some experience with helping congregations move toward healing when I was serving as an interim pastor. Now, it was time to take those lessons and apply them in a different context, that of a "regular" call. I had little idea how deeply I would be moved and changed by the makeover that occurred at Messiah. How was I changed? I was challenged to grow my own giving, to believe that a relaxed and collaborative approach could be a form of strong leadership, and that stepping out in faith could be exhilarating, terrifying, and liberating.

Perhaps one of the best lessons I learned was one that I wish for many of my fellow pastors: I'm dispensable. When a person realizes they're dispensable, they are freed to stop believing that everything depends on them; that realization is also a great antidote to the disease of "important-itis" that can afflict us. There's much more room for God to work when we pastors have the good sense to stay out of the way. I hope that reading this story of one person's ministry journey allows readers to bring light and air into their ministry settings and to not be afraid when God calls you to do more, give more, and be more than you might have ever thought possible. When a congregation is willing to let God jump-start it, amazing things really can happen.

To continue the story, consider the following:

"Pastor Beth, I've just got to come to church every week because I never know what might happen!" So said a delighted and active octogenarian of the transformational ministry happening at his church. Let's call him Erv. He went on, describing the thrill he got from seeing children assisting in worship, families ushering together, beginning musicians sharing their music, and "them (sic) little kids singing like that!" What made Erv's enthusiasm especially meaningful was his unwavering support of his church, the congregation's first female pastor, and his understanding of what it meant to be a good "churchman," in the best sense of that old term.

Deepening Erv's joy was his memory of the difficult days in this congregation, the hard times. He recalled, "Pastor, there were some Sundays we weren't sure if we were going to see each other the next week because we didn't know if the doors would be open."

Because of various economic and staffing factors that collided somewhat like the perfect storm, the congregation had been in decline for a while. When I came, the congregation was faced with the decision to either build a new building or close the doors. This was a dramatic opportunity for faith and renewal! The building was just the beginning, though. The folks at Messiah ended up doing a whole lot more, too. They were transformed from a congregation that wasn't sure they had a future to one recognized by the national church for their approach to ministry and outreach. They started to see themselves differently once they had a new facility. Not only was their self-esteem on the upswing, but after the building was up, they had a facility they felt good about, and inviting others to "come and see" spurred outreach and evangelism efforts. With the new, accessible facility, they also hosted community and synodical events, had youth lock-ins, invited the school to use their facility for the annual fundraising talent show that previously had been held in a gymnasium, sponsored what became an annual dinner, and so on. Thus, a makeover for mission and ministry was born. The story of how they reached this point in their life together is instructive and, I hope, inspiring.

Chapter 2

Iowa Skepticism Meets Iowa Determination

"Can we build it? Yes we can!"
— Bob the Builder, PBS TV show

Had anyone told that little congregation and me that we would be recognized within a decade by the national church body as a model for ministry in action, they would have been met with good old-fashioned Iowa skepticism. After all, this was a congregation with a $22,500 yearly budget; it could barely meet its monthly commitments and its self-esteem had plummeted. Yet the congregation had faith.

Assisting the congregation in its faithfulness was the healing ministry of a semi-retired pastor and his wife. From 1991-1995, Pastor Ray and Elaine Ehlers ministered at Messiah after a couple of pastorates that hadn't quite clicked. At that time, the congregation's future was bleak. Together, Ray and Elaine worked over the course of four years to restore the congregation's battered ego and led them to the point of talking about building. Generating that vision also prompted the congregation to create a call committee charged with finding a pastor suitable to the tasks of building and transformational ministry.

My family and I came on board in mid-1996. When we started, my husband, a journalist, set about to revamp the publications, which played a substantial role in the congregation's renewal. Our seven-month-old daughter was one of the few children in church. When visiting with families with children, I was able to say, "Don't ever worry about your children acting up in church. Chances are the preacher's kid has already done something like that!" And so she had. When our daughter was a toddler, for example, she got away from her father in the sanctuary once and started doing laps around the pews in her stocking feet!

Another time, on Maundy Thursday, she sneaked away during the prayers and ended up sitting next to her mother on the "pastor's pew" up front. The congregation didn't object. If anything, they saw more joy in it than their pastor did. But this was a congregation that could recall when they had few children in worship. That memory was seared into them every quiet Sunday when there were no outbursts, no crying children, no Cheerios clattering on wooden pews or spilling on the floor.

Support and Setbacks

Eventually, though, the volume level started changing. Families with children were worshiping at Messiah. And as the congregation started moving forward, sounds of construction echoed up and down the streets after the groundbreaking ceremony in May, 1998. Backhoes, trucks, cement pumpers, and construction workers would eventually fill the site. But getting to that point involved planning, persistence, and some re-thinking.

After a generous, $50,000 no-strings-attached gift from an anonymous donor catapulted the congregation into serious consideration of the building process in October of 1996, members formed the Building Vision Task Force in January. The group began gathering ideas and resources for the new facility. The theme around which everything became organized was timely, too, because the twenty-first century was soon to arrive. Accordingly, Messiah planned to build "A New Church for a New Century." The group presented their findings in May of 1997, along with a recommended time-table for financing and building. Those meetings moved the plan forward, and by November 1997, a topographical survey had been conducted, extra land acquired, an architect of the ELCA hired, and a capital appeal readied.

Additional financial good news came from two area congregations celebrating significant anniversaries. In the spring of 1998, St. Paul's Lutheran, Waverly, as part of its 125th anniversary celebration received a "love offering" for Messiah and gave the young congregation $16,000 toward the new building. In the fall, St. John Lutheran, Nashua, in honor of its centennial anniversary, gave a $10,000 love offering as well. Both churches had played significant roles in my life, and now they both wanted to help. I had served St. John as interim pastor prior to accepting the call to serve in Janesville. St. Paul's was the church I joined after I married my husband and I had been there during my college days as well. The support of both these churches — as well as smaller financial gifts from other area congregations — bolstered the members of Messiah. It is terrific to be on the receiving end of love offerings, but they're also great for the congregation that makes such a gift. To give of ourselves for the sake of others, instead of hoarding the gifts God has so richly blessed us with, helps keep congregations outwardly directed, and that makes for healthier congregations. Moreover, the generosity and belief these area congregations had in us was inspiring.

For a while, all was moving along well. A groundbreaking date had been set for May 3, 1998. The Mission Builders of the ELCA, retired folks with construction experience who travel to places where there is a need for their expertise, were interested in the project. Then, sadly, the first architect's vision and the congregation's vision didn't mesh. The architect had designed a more traditional building, not reflective of our "New Church for a New Century" theme. Adding to the setback was the cost: half again what the congregation had budgeted. The congregation once more faced obstacles in their quest to build a permanent facility. Would these latest glitches stand in the way? Hardly.

Keep Going

Remarkably, at each step along the way, the congregation voted unanimously to keep going. Even when the initial cost of extra land was higher than church members had hoped, even when the discouragement with the architect was palpable, even when building projections were much higher than anticipated, even when the time-table seemed mired down because of the initial architectural upset, the congregation said "go." The newsletter recorded the next steps:

> *At an information meeting following the April 19, 1998, worship service, members voiced their wishes informally and nearly all who spoke urged the [Building Committee and the Finance Committee] to move ahead and get the facility built. President Scott Gasner said, "We've got the message. We don't intend to drop the ball."*

With the strong support of the congregation, the project moved forward. Many may wonder what helped the congregation keep moving, even in the face of the challenges and disappointments. All along, the building committee was honest with the congregation about what had happened, and that sort of transparency was invaluable. When a second calculation of the capital campaign results revealed an addition error, for example, the person doing the calculating apologized, said he'd made a mistake with the earlier calculation and announced the revised total. The difference was not a small amount, but the people took it in stride, thanked him for his efforts, and just kept moving. There was such a sense of shared responsibility, and such enthusiasm for the project, that no one was eager to be derailed. That sort of approach carried us. There was no finger-pointing, as happens occasionally, but instead a collective willingness to acknowledge mistakes and then move on.

Another thing that we found helpful was the belief that the time had finally come to get done what the charter members had hoped for so long ago. We still had living charter members worshiping with us, so there was a desire to finally accomplish what had been put in motion. Call it a sense of obligation or an awareness of history, but whatever it was figured into the thinking when we had obstacles. Knowing how close we had come in the past, we did not want to have to stop now. It was also important that the present members remember that those who had come before them had faith enough to get a church started, and that now we were the ones to build for those who would come after us.

There was a strong belief that God was both calling us into the future and equipping us with the courage and the strength needed to meet the challenges. There was still enthusiasm for the project because the leadership of the congregation was confident that God was leading us, even in the dark days.

Through all of the challenges, we kept talking to each other, hosting informational meetings, and keeping the people informed. That sort of partnership, undergirded by the grace and strength of God, was essential to the ultimate success of the entire building project and allowed the congregation to forge ahead in faith and mission. After firing the first architect, the building committee met with a local design/build firm, and new plans were drawn up. People got on board with the new facility, ground was broken, and work on the new facility commenced in the fall of 1998 with the goal being to move in on Easter Sunday, 1999.

Building Tells the Story

As the footings went in and the building went up, it was as if that line from the movie Field of Dreams — "If you build it they will come" — came to life for Messiah, too. After years of talking about a new facility, the congregation now had tangible evidence of its intent. Piles of dirt, the rumble of heavy equipment, and a steel frame signaled our commitment to building a new facility. We were building a "New Church for a New Century." Building happened at just the right time it seemed, also, because the current facility began serving notice of its age. In succession, there was a gas leak near the kitchen stove, a crabby yard sign that refused to light up, a leaky toilet, an air-conditioning breakdown as hot weather abated, and a leak under the kitchen sinks. After one more winter in the old church, the furnace gave out too.

Almost daily, people observed progress on the new building. The footings were soon joined by a foundation, utility hook-ups, a steel frame and studs, a roof, and insulation. Excitement abounded. The committees worked hard, also, choosing carpeting, pews, light fixtures, and determining what would make the trek from the old building to the new. Progress continued at a pace that made moving in on Easter Sunday, 1999, possible.

During that time, the congregation readied itself for the move. Maundy Thursday and Good Friday included worship times as well as opportunities to physically move items into the new space. Easter Sunday began with a farewell to the old building followed by a processional to the new building. The new facility, facing east and thus basking in the rising sun, welcomed an overflow crowd to its sanctuary. Following a festive worship service celebrating the risen Christ, many people stayed to enjoy a continental breakfast served by the junior high and high school students and their families, who had become increasingly involved as things began to turn around at Messiah. Many people also browsed around the rooms in the new building.

Work on the building was not done, however. There were interior finishing projects and exterior landscaping projects to be finished. The sound system, fireplace, and stained glass came later, as did a parking lot, but the hurdle of building a church that was meant to be a church had been cleared.

There was more than building going on at Messiah, though. The congregation paid attention to its worship life, to education and youth ministry, to social causes, community events, and Christmas care for a family in need. As people began to "live into" the new space, programming for mission evolved, too, especially since we now had a welcoming, accessible space that we were pleased to share with the community. Perhaps nowhere was the significance of new possibilities more apparent than the ways in which children were included to an even greater degree in the life of the parish.

Chapter 3

From Snowforts to Glowsticks

"It was great being a kid at Messiah."
— Ariana Gremmels Olson, age 9

As the congregation grew, so did the number of families with children at worship. Because the congregation had known a dry spell when few children were active in worship, it was more than willing to include children in various capacities. Children ushered with their families. Young children served as basket-bearers for the empty communion cups. Children and parents were encouraged to read the lessons together during worship. This kind of participation may seem commonplace now, but when this was written in 2014, there were (and likely still are) some congregations who rarely let young children have so prominent a role in the worship life of the congregation. What a difference that role made for Messiah! So welcome did children know they were that one afternoon, two of the fourth-grade students came up after school in the winter to visit with me.

"Pastor Beth, we've just built a snow fort down in the field. Will you come and say a prayer in it with us?" There was a house blessing in the Occasional Services book, but no snow-fort references. Nevertheless, off I went, trudging through the snow-covered field with Dana and Mitch. This snow-fort blessing led to a conversation at Sunday school in the following weeks about housing. Mitch and Dana wondered if the Sunday school kids could help build homes for people that didn't have them. Wow! Those two young leaders rallied people: they made posters, spoke at worship, used their Sunday school offering money, and got the congregation to kick in some of the Lenten offering. Together, the congregation made a combined gift of $400 to the local Habitat for Humanity chapter. It was an amazing event in the saga of this congregational makeover, and it was only one of many things that happened because children knew they were welcome, their ideas were valued, and their contributions encouraged.

Being Child and Family-Friendly

Love it or lament it, but the days of "children being seen and not heard" were on their way out. The congregation welcomed the noises of children because they could remember when having children in worship was an irregular occurrence. As light and air filtered back into the congregation, one of the things we did was seek out ways to be child and family-friendly.

Being child and family-friendly isn't rocket science or brain surgery. At the heart of a ministry that welcomes children are people who will pay attention, who will take the time to listen, who will look at the world through a child's eyes. Having a young child myself, I was able to look around and see if we had kid-friendly things such as activity bags for worship, worship bulletins for children, and ways to involve children in the ministry of the congregation.

It helped that others had children of similar ages, too, because they wanted the same things for their children that I did for mine: for church to be a place of welcome. And it helped that we had some wonderful members of the congregation who acted as "adopted grandparents" for the younger set. They sat together in worship, enjoyed treats together, and had get-togethers apart from church.

The other thing that was tremendously valuable was that the more seasoned members of the church welcomed the presence of kids. We capitalized on this and paired up "friends in faith" and had the older folks sit with the younger folks, even doing a craft project or something. And we tore a page from the Total Family Sunday School program assembled by Rich Melheim and Faith Inkubators. We used the multi-generational approach for Lenten services and let the fellowship unfold. Teens and adults sat together at the fellowship hall tables for supper and conversation; the little kids hauled out the big pillows and played on the floor or sat with each other.

Together, we created places and spaces for children to get involved. In the new building, the children were invited to decorate the nursery room walls with their handprints; adult volunteers painted the children's hands and then helped them put their prints on the walls. The congregation also collected items for Lutheran World Relief kits, sent home World Hunger Appeal collection coin boxes and calendars, made seasonal banners to hang on the walls, and prayed for families by name in worship each week.

How did the congregation make all this happen? An attitude of openness and the knowledge that by getting kids involved, the parents were likely to be more involved, too, fostered participation, but it wasn't any one approach that generated youth involvement. Sometimes, parents and/or grandparents asked if their child/grandchild could help, and we found ways to involve them. Sometimes, it was a name change that allowed families to get involved. The more formal "Altar Guild," for example, became the Worship Prep Team, and families were encouraged to set up the worship space. In some cases, the name change reflected what was happening behind the scenes anyway, because the parents often hauled along the kids to help anyhow.

The congregation council also had a hand in making things happen. Often, the questions about involvement came their way, and so we asked how we can keep making the church child and family friendly. Some said, "Let's get the kids involved with this," with everything from clean-up days to special music. It also helped that so many people loved the children and smiled when they saw the kids ushering or holding the communion baskets and getting involved. In short, to encourage children, we paid attention and then we asked, offered, invited, and responded.

Eventually, Messiah added a youth director to its staff. Our proximity to a local Evangelical Lutheran Church in America (ELCA) college made it easy to advertise, interview, and eventually bring in someone with gifts and skills to continue building the youth program. The congregational commitment to youth was another component in making transformation happen. With the guidance and enthusiasm of the youth director, we organized domestic and international service trips, engaged in local projects, hosted various youth events in which friends were welcome, and had youth Bible studies and conversation.

Children were delighted one Christmas Eve to discover that something other than parental-anxiety-inducing candles awaited them. Andrea Sherwood, Messiah's youth director, had seen a flyer for glow-sticks and so she ordered a boxful to share with the younger members at candlelight services. What a hit! And what a great way to include children and help parents have a little less stress during the Christmas craziness that is too much a part of modern culture. A great example of coming to church because you never know what might happen! And the commitment to making Messiah youth and family-friendly encouraged creativity and generated an almost playful spirit that spilled over into relationships and activities. In short, people realized one could have fun at church, as well as have an enriching and meaningful experience. Those sorts of reactions weren't mutually exclusive.

Playing on Sunday Mornings

With being child and family friendly, we also became increasingly aware of the "sports on Sundays juggernaut" that puts so many families in an awkward bind on Sunday mornings.

As with many congregations, Messiah was not immune to the conflicts created by that reality.

Kids are overwhelmed with opportunities to play in this event or that tournament, many spread over a Saturday and Sunday. Families spend big bucks on equipment, uniforms, food, and hotel bills. Parents routinely drive two, four, even six hours or more to take their offspring to various venues. That kind of time together in the car may be valuable family time, but this author laments the loss of church community that many of those families may be missing.

On more than one occasion, I went out on that limb and found there were very few willing to have a conversation about the role of sports and church and keeping Sunday morning holy. For many, the new worship space is the court/mat/gymnasium of this meet or that event and the pews are known as bleachers. That saddens me. How often the church has been a source of strength, comfort, challenge, and joy precisely because it connected me not only to a caring congregation, but with the almighty God of the universe, both transcendent and incarnate. Even so, I once had a mother tell me that her daughter would love to be at church, but she didn't want to disappoint her team. Well... what about God's team? The attitude of church as "second fiddle" or "back-up plan" is disappointing, and it may be more permanent than many of us want to admit. This, too, may be more noticeable in smaller congregations due to the percentage and the impact such absences create.

More Questions than Answers

If part of the appeal of church is that it is countercultural, how are pastors to address the issue? And how are people to help one another see that transformation doesn't mean conducting business as usual?

That leads to another question: how do pastors speak up about such issues? If we raise the questions, are we perceived as whining? Are the questions perceived as law? Are pastors perceived as begging for an offering envelope? Are we perceived as doing our job and adhering to our letter of call? Are we reminding people that God asks to be first in our lives? Should pastors just let such topics alone, recognize that people will come to church when they can (or want to), and be content with that?

For a personal perspective, I also know how convenient it was (and is) to be able to stop by the local 24-hour grocery store on my way home from church to pick up a quart of milk or that last ingredient for Sunday dinner. Would I advocate a return to earlier days, where everything closed up on Sundays? No. Would I advocate for doing away with youth sporting programs? No.

Whatever we do, it seems to this writer that we want to make sure that we consistently offer the best we can to our people, recognizing that church is but one item on a very full buffet menu of life events to choose from, so that when they do come, they have a meaningful experience that strengthens and nurtures them, one that makes them feel as though they want to come back.

Chapter 4

Worship, Welcome, and a Relaxed Fit

"Pastor Beff [sic], *we've got more customers!"*
— Madyson, age 4

Walking into church after having been away for a while can be daunting. Walking into a new church without prior church experience can be overwhelming. We discovered in our years together that our church provided an easier entry point both for those who had been away and those who had little church background, the unchurched, and the "de-churched," I'll call them. What's a "de-churched" person? It's someone who had been active in a church but who, for whatever reason, got turned off and stepped out for a while — sometimes weeks, but more likely months or years. Maybe a pastor rubbed them wrong, maybe something happened at some time in history, maybe they just needed a break. For whatever reason, they've been turned off from church, de-churched.

What made entry at Messiah less intimidating? Access was one thing. There was very little confusion over where to enter the church. The main doors were obvious. Once a person got inside, finding the sanctuary was easy: It was immediately off to the left and very visible. Most everyone's been in churches where a person almost needs a GPS system to find one's way around. Even with signage!

Besides the easy-to-identify worship space at Messiah, there was at least one person (besides the pastor) present to welcome people. Pastorally, I made it a point to have all my worship prep work done before worshipers showed up so that I could mix and mingle, and welcome unfamiliar faces. Thankfully, however, the welcoming task was not solely mine. This congregation was welcoming to people well before I showed up, and they remain a welcoming congregation.

To welcome without hovering is an artful extension of hospitality. Here's some of how it went at Messiah: People entering were directed to the guest book, shown the coat closet, and invited to stay for coffee and treats after church, often by one of the friendly folks who extended Messiah hospitality. During coffee, newcomers weren't left to sit by themselves, either. Someone from the parish took the initiative to introduce themselves to our guests. I tried to keep an eye on things as I was able, but knowing guestwere being cared for by the congregation was a great gift. Some of those folks even took their association with Messiah a step further and became active, engaged members of the congregation.

New people are an important part of a congregation's growth and life. Having visitors means that congregations are doing their work and getting the word out about their ministry, and it also means that there's a "buzz" being generated that intrigues people and draws them to your ministry. Curiosity makes them want to see what's going on, which can be a terrific asset if you have good things going on that you want to share.

Inside the Sanctuary

The actual worship service itself provided numerous opportunities for welcome. Even before the congregation moved into the new facility, we offered children's bulletins and crayons to the younger set, as well as having regular children's messages during worship. This may sound old for some readers, and some of you may have been doing these things for a long time. If so, congratulations! For us, these were new ventures. They were well-received, and families quickly came to realize that their children were welcome at church.

Having a child myself, I felt free to tell the parents when their children fussed or cried or acted up, "You don't ever have to worry about your children in church. After all, we can remember when we didn't have children in worship." That was greeted with a smile, and the older folks of the congregation echoed the sentiment. It remains a sweet memory that my own daughter was the recipient of the special love of her "church grandparents." For her, Messiah came to mean sitting with them every Sunday and enjoying the treats and affection they showered upon her. If only all children were so fortunate!

To be a welcoming and accessible church also meant being unconventional on occasion. While lilies are often a staple on Easter morning, butterfly balloons didn't grace too many sanctuaries that I was aware of. But they did at Messiah, thanks to one of the other mothers who thought the balloons would be a lovely addition to our Easter celebration. Mary was right. In that same spirit was the use of glowsticks instead of candles for little kids at the candlelight service on Christmas Eve.

I also believed that worship needed to be done well, with care, grace, and attention to detail. Bulletins were easy to follow, liturgy sung crisply, and new hymns introduced occasionally, too. I recalled the advice of my preaching professor, Bud Buchheim, who said, "Preach with the Bible in one hand and the newspaper in the other." That sage advice led to what I hoped were relevant and challenging homilies that encouraged the congregation to connect faith and life, to make the Sunday/Monday connection. Prayers also reflected the global community we live in and helped expand the worldview of those assembled, hopefully sensitizing us to the larger world we were part of and helping see how far-reaching the ministry of the congregation, synod, and ELCA was.

Another important component to our Sunday morning approach was flexibility, especially as exemplified by a beatitude on an old poster, "Blessed are the flexible for they will not be bent out of shape." Things don't always go as expected on Sunday mornings, and it's important that pastors not pass along their anxieties to the congregation. Being able to laugh at myself proved helpful on more than one occasion: lifting up the chalice while saying the words of institution for the bread, for example, or being able to make a witty remark about Lutheran aerobics with our standing up and sitting down. The more important point of being flexible and "rolling with it" when unexpected things happened was that people knew they didn't need to be perfect at Messiah. There was breathing room, and thus room for participation by a host of people instead.

Preaching and Life in Community

It's a holy privilege to be a pastor. As preachers, we are blessed to come to know and to bear the burdens of the people we are in community with. I recall the young man whose wife had been diagnosed with a rare and deadly disease and the middle-aged woman with a brain tumor who probably wouldn't live to see her grandchildren grow up. I remember the widows and widowers so despondent over the loss of their beloved that they sank into depression and despair, and the pensioners who wondered how they would pay their bills as the cost of gas and heating oil continued to rise. I marveled at the farmers who still engaged in that great act of faith even in the face of changing weather and volatile markets. And I listened to the young people who were trying to figure out who they were, juggling classes, jobs, and co-curricular activities, dealing with pressures and temptations many of us who are older never faced when we were growing up. In those most painful places of peoples' lives, pastors bring words of hope, forgiveness, power, grace, and peace. Pastors are privileged to carry and bear the rituals of the church into the most joyous, painful, and sacred places of peoples' lives.

In his book Finally Comes the Poet, Walter Brueggemann cautions pastors against letting the gospel be "an old habit among us," something that becomes "comfortable" and "leaves us unbothered."

Because of the tremendous pains, hopes, and expectations people bring to worship week after week, worship leaders need to create an atmosphere where people sense they are cared for, where the attention to detail and the awareness to the communal life unfolds in as seamless a way as possible as often as possible, so that worship can fill people and sustain them for the coming week. Worship done well is another extension of pastoral care.

When I was growing up, getting to church was rarely worshipful. There were six kids to get ready and the church was four miles away. The church bell was often ringing as we pulled into the parking lot. Was it any wonder the eight of us usually sat toward the front of the church? Life has not slowed down for today's families, either. There's still often a mad dash for families with children to get to church, grab the children's resources,

shepherd them down the aisle, and then settle in. S
getting to church is like crossing the finish line of a
Worship leaders help families more than they realize
having their act together when families are ready tc
Worship should start on time and be well-orchestrated and done in a timely fashion, because worship done well creates space for contemplation, interaction, and communion with God and each other.

In Life Together, German theologian, pastor and martyr Dietrich Bonhoeffer lifts up the blessing and privilege of Christian community. In one instance he says, "It is by the grace of God that a congregation is permitted to gather visibly in this world to share God's word and sacrament."1 Not only is it by God's grace that congregations gather, it is in God's grace they do so and, hopefully, God's grace that is celebrated too.

God's grace was also celebrated when we implemented mid-week Lenten services. Since we were basically starting over, we didn't feel compelled to use a traditional service. When we did re-institute Lenten services, we did so with a twist. There was a family component to each gathering. Conversation starters on the tables, crafts that tied in with the theme, and family devotions aided our observance. Some of the old-timers raised their eyebrows, and this kind of Lenten programming might not have gone over in every congregation, but it worked here. It worked in part because when one has faced dying, one is willing to be a little bolder, to risk a little bit more. Or, as former ELCA presiding bishop H. George Anderson once said, "There can be no resurrection without a death." Lenten services were resurrected and became part of the spring worship cycle once again, after a long hiatus, and extended faith families were formed as we gathered for meal and worship.

Warm Welcomes

When a congregation wants to be welcoming, it's important to publicly speak and model that welcome every Sunday. We did that by inviting people who were looking for a church home to "consider Messiah." It wasn't a high-powered sales tactic, just a simple invitation to think about Messiah as a possible worship home, stay for coffee and conversation and then come back if they were so inclined. Worshipers were invited to bring a friend to worship, children knew there were bulletins and crayons for them, and everyone was welcome to stay for coffee, fellowship, and education.

Other opportunities for hospitality came through non-Sunday services such as funerals and weddings. The impression we gave through these services also created connections and opened windows of opportunities for people to check out our congregation. More than one person ended up joining Messiah eventually after their initial exposure at some of these occasional services.

One pitfall we tried to avoid was assuming people knew the "secret codes" of worship: hymn numbers and liturgy numbers, for example, or front part and back part of the book, or later on, what color book we were in (Green? Blue? Cranberry? Other?). More than once during the service, I signaled where we were in the liturgy by announcing page numbers. It's a seemingly small thing, but it cleared up a lot of the confused looks I saw from behind the altar. Also, we realized that the people in the very front row didn't always know to look under their pews for books, so we'd leave books on the pews.

Just like relaxed jeans can be more enjoyable to wear, so a more relaxed approach to worship proved effective, and people didn't have to feel nervous about whether they were "doing everything right." People returning to church have enough stuff to contend with without having to feel awkward about not knowing where they are, and sensitivity on the part of the worship leaders goes a long way toward easing anxiety.

Lighthearted and Unflappable

It also helps to be able to take a light-hearted view of those various unexpected "moments" that arise in worship, especially when children are involved. At the first Easter vigil in the new church, for example, people got a little more than they anticipated. The vigil is a solemn service, with lots of scripture, darkness, and church rituals. It was also a relatively new service at Messiah. This particular year, a little girl, about four, familiar with the church and the pastor and comfortable talking with adults, waited in the narthex. While she looked around, the doors opened and people entered. "Pastor Beff," she exclaimed, "we've got more customers!" I should have had a clue then that this might be a livelier service than anticipated.

This same little one had brought with her a dyed egg in a basket for church that night. Since the crowd was slim, the sanctuary fairly dark, and the scripture passages numerous, I thought it might be helpful to the children if they gathered around as we told the scripture stories. The youngster was determined to tell me that her egg had a chick in it and that it would hatch one day and be a sign of new life. We didn't go into details, but she got her point across. The service went on, but not without some giggles.

That episode also reminds me that in the pastoral ministry, it helps to be unflappable, to be equipped to handle most anything that comes up, because you never know when a bat may swoop into an education meeting or when a frog may find its way into the kitchen; when children will say the darndest things, as they do often at the children's message time. Being unflappable is also invaluable when people share those most painful parts of their lives with the pastor, those stories of families in crisis, of abusive relationships, of kids experimenting with sex, drugs, alcohol that happen in all kinds of communities and all kinds of congregations. What people need at such times is a non-judgmental, attentive listener who is able to float with whatever happens. Registering shock or horror or disgust can be a sure-fire way to close down a conversation.

The other element of listening to those heart-wrenching details of broken lives, broken homes, broken vows, broken boundaries, is recognizing that we come face-to-face with sin. We who have faced our own darkness also know that there is nothing that another person can say that will be so horrible that we cannot bear it. Few things in life are as daunting as looking at our own sinfulness and discovering the power of the crucified and risen Christ to heal it. The early church father Athanasius said that what Christ has redeemed, Christ has healed.

People in pain looking for their own inner healing and transformation don't need pious platitudes filled with do-goodisms or the quick judgmentalism that spring too easily to the mouth. What they need is the story of the flesh and blood Savior who died that we might have new life. And pastors are privileged to bring those wonderful words into those awful places, words of grace and hope, of forgiveness and peace, of new life and possibility, of joy and restoration. Encouraging people to give their grief and pain over to God is one of the most moving parts of pastoral ministry, especially when done in the context of the service of individual confession. The death to self allows the spirit of resurrection renewal to be unleashed. It is a fearful, holy, and awesome thing to come face to face with such death and to allow God to bring about the restoration and transformation such actions invariably invite.

---

1. Dietrich Bonhoeffer, *Life Together* (San Francisco: Harper and Row, 1954), p. 18.

Chapter 5

The Body of Christ, Living Care Packages

"Care for God's people, bear their burdens, and do not betray their confidence."
  — Service of Ordination, LBW Occasional Services Book

When a person trains to be a pastor in the Lutheran Church, part of their education involves some sort of clinical pastoral education (CPE). It's usually a summer in an institutional setting such as a hospital, nursing home, or mental health institute. One is with a group with other student chaplains and guided by a supervisor. This training is designed to help pastors-to-be gain some valuable real-world experience dealing with emergencies, families in crisis, and the medical community. It is also a time for pastoral candidates to explore their own emotions and reactions to various situations. Pastors learn how to process some of their own life-events with the goal of being better equipped to assist parishioners. Chances are, every pastor who has gone through this training has memorable stories about "learning the ropes."

From Student Chaplain to Community Pastor
It's one thing, though, to be a student chaplain for three months and be paged to assist a group of strangers in an emergency. It's quite another to be the pastor in the midst of the community when people you've come to know and love over a period of time experience the heartaches of life. Then the privilege of serving as a pastor is apparent. I recall a couple in their thirties. They were pregnant and ready to welcome another child into their family. One day at lunch, I got a phone call from the expectant — and upset — mother, "Pastor, can you come? We think something's wrong with the baby. We haven't felt it move at all for a long time now." I told

I'd meet them at the hospital. Their fears proved to be well-founded. Tests confirmed that the baby had died. Because of the boy's developmental age, the woman would have to go through the birth process. Few things strike me as being more horrible to experience than the labor of bringing a dead child into the world. "Pastor, I'd like if you could stay," she said. So I stayed, we held hands and prayed. Later, I held one of those very same hands as she tearfully and painfully brought forth the dead fruit from her womb. The child looked perfect. It fit into its father's hand. We buried the child, and a community came together to care for this family.

The Lutheran theology of suffering means we believe that because God in Christ was willing to fully enter into the suffering of humanity and redeem it, we, too, can be unafraid of the darkness and ugliness of human existence. I don't believe a person can be an effective pastor and be afraid of people's pain. We are privileged to bring a word of God, of hope, peace, and power, into those most painful moments in people's lives; that itself is transformational ministry.

Often, after one has been established in a community, others not directly connected with the church will invite the pastor into those places, too. These meetings are great opportunities to extend your church's welcome! The call came in the middle of the night, for example, wondering if I could go and sit with a family whose grandchild was in distress. They weren't members of the parish, but because of connections with neighbors and the community I was invited into the emergency room with them. Another time, the the volunteer fire department asked me to be part of a critical incident debriefing. Before reaching that point, though, a person has to earn the trust and respect of the people, and that means staying put for a while. Transformational ministry takes time and care. Too many pastors make the mistake of staying too short a time period. (Yes, some overstay their welcome too; knowing when to leave is an art!) But recognizing that it takes at least three to five years to get established in a place is a healthy reminder. I remember when a bigger church in the area had a pastoral vacancy two or three years into my ministry. A couple of people came to me and said, essentially, "I suppose you'll be looking to leave for the bigger place, huh?" I reassured them I wasn't. There was still plenty to be done where I was. But by staying, I also passed some sort of test in their eyes. The lure of the big city tugs at some, for various reasons, but there can be — and is — great reward serving in smaller settings too.

Another part of earning community trust is being visible in the community: ball games, musical events, local suppers are all terrific times to mix and mingle, as well as learn more about the people one has been called to live among. It might even lead to being asked to sit in the dunk-tank for a 4-H fundraiser. Thank goodness it was a sunny day and the shift was only thirty minutes!

During the course of ministry at Messiah, I was asked to officiate at funerals for those only marginally connected with a church and for those with no church affiliation. Though I naturally preferred church funerals to funeral home services, both were opportunities to bring a word from God to people. Sometimes those random encounters bore the fruit of discipleship later on, when people came for worship because of something said at a funeral or because of the welcome they experienced. Once, another church's pastor (from a denomination that does not ordain women) and I even shared funeral duties, which still strikes me as remarkable, but then transformational ministry itself provides remarkable moments. Transformational ministry in small towns ripples out in unexpected ways.

What is not so remarkable is how the commitment to caring generates ministry and growth opportunities; people want to know that someone else cares about them, that there is someone willing to listen to them, pray with them, and bring the word of God to the bedside of their critically ill grandchild, their dying sister, their husband or wife, their grandparent or friend.

I can still see the surprised look on one farmer's face when I showed up at his place after a devastating hail storm came through and shredded the crops. This barrel-chested, stoic German farmer had tears in his eyes; he was astonished that his preacher had come out to visit. Why was that so hard to believe? Care itself is transformative.

The Privilege of Pastoring

Being with people in their pain also affords opportunities to claim one's identity as pastor. By that I mean using the gifts of the call to live into one's pastoral identity. People who stopped by for conversation and consolation soon learned they rarely left the pastor's office without a prayer. For that part of my pastoral identity, I am indebted to another seminary professor, Duane Priebe, who taught me how to pray. I was going through a particularly rough patch during my second year of seminary, confronting my own demons and the dark power of human sinfulness; this wise, gentle pastor shepherded me through my anger, pain, and rage by listening patiently, guiding skillfully, and praying boldly. No matter my state of mind, he prayed.

Those prayers held me together when lots of other things were falling apart. They also set the stage for those times when I was the one praying. That is another example of the power of care that transforms people. The experience of being prayed for is almost too powerful for words to convey.

Beyond that, the experience of being prayed for in the context of genuine pastoral care has shaped my pastoral ministry. Whether it's praying with people gathered around the bed of their loved one in ICU or sharing the Commendation of the Dying service with them, the prayers and words we offer up can touch that deep emotional level that connects people most intimately to God. It also often allows them to shed the tears they try so mightily to keep at bay. In a holy and life-giving way, our prayers can articulate the theology that so shapes us. In a world in love with thinking that everything that glitters is gold, pastors enter into another's suffering and remind them that through the suffering of Christ crucified and risen, God brings life from death, light from darkness, beauty from ugliness, and creation from chaos. To utter those words in prayer in the presence of a wounded human being is both humbling and powerful, and it reminds me of the pastoral privilege we who serve have.

Another privilege of the pastoral office is witnessing the love and devotion of many families: such as the tender embrace of a grandson moving his dying grandmother from chair to bed, the emotional decisions of families to stop life support, the joyous reunions of those long separated, or the tender care of a new addition to the family. There are endless stories along the spectrum of life and death; to share these journeys as pastor is a gift.

Perhaps because of some of the calls I've had, though, I've heard stories from parishioners about how ministry was not tended, or people were selectively cared for, or dictatorial decisions were made by my fellow clergy that have saddened me or just downright angered me. I have heard of how pastors have betrayed the office of ministry or the trust that was given to them by the people — and that doesn't even include the clergy sexual abuse scandal, which is a whole other topic. I'm talking more about those who carry such a sense of self-importance that they're not very pleasant to be around, or those who are heavy-handed in their approach to theology as if they have to show people that they're the "educated ones" in the communities.

I've been a pastor for twenty years, and while I don't have a lot of the answers, I've heard so many stories from parishioners about badly-behaving pastors that the faithfulness of people who keep coming to church after an ugly situation still amazes me. Many know what some pastors seem to forget: This is God's church. The people also know this corollary: Pastors come and go, so we will likely outlast them. But what about the damage the pastors do in the meantime? What about the generations they turn off because of their heavy-handed or high-brow ways?

Now, fellow pastors who are reading this, before you get on your high horse and get all honked off, understand that I'm probably not talking about you. If you're loving your people and letting them love you, chances are you're okay. (See next section.) But if you're having some trouble, maybe you need to look at yourself, too. I get it that there are "alligators" in the congregation who'd just as soon snap at you as support you, but sometimes, if we're honest with ourselves, we bring the trouble on ourselves.

I understand there can be dysfunction in a congregation just as there can be in a family, though it's multiplied and perhaps more deeply ingrained because of the generational overlap existent in some congregations. Even so, we are called to serve the people of God. Ministry is still a privilege. We are let into some of the most sacred places in peoples' lives to bring a word of hope, forgiveness, joy, peace. It's a privilege we best keep in our sights, as it helps with the humility necessary to do our jobs well and effectively.

Love the People and Let Them Love You
Pastors also need to be willing to receive the love and care of their congregations. Some of the best advice I received about being a pastor came from a retired minister, Ray Ehlers, whose advice was, "Love the people and let them love you." I think of a story a colleague, Pr. Donnita Moeller, shared years ago. She was pastoring in a Hispanic community in the South. She was invited to a potluck and though her palate was more Scandinavian than Hispanic, she ate the food the people had brought. She, too, had passed a test of community. "They welcomed my ministry," she related, "because I ate their food." When people know you care about them, it allows them to trust you. That trust leads to doing good things for God together.

We also shared meals together at Messiah. The youth and their families hosted a Seder Supper one year. Great fellowship and more than a few laughs came during preparation time. When it was meal time itself, the generations sat together in a way resembling a family gathering; we even had a "little kids" table for the youngest among us that day.

Eucharist was another of those shared meals. In the old church, we lined up in a straight row across the front of the altar area. A pleasant change in the new facility was the chance to gather in a semi-circle around the altar on smaller occasion services such as Ash Wednesday or Maundy Thursday. The intimacy there reflected the care in community many felt. For "regular" Sundays, we communed processional-style. Looking one's congregation in the eye, knowing their scars and secrets, their joys and dreams, generates humility and gratitude. The intimacy communion affords is striking, and the joy communal meals affords is liberating. But communal meals create deeper connections, also. Studies have shown families who share meals together have kids who get into trouble less often, are better students, and are more secure in dealing with life. The act of sitting around the table and talking about the day, troubleshooting problems, discussing strategies, planning for the future, and even dreaming about possibilities better equips young people to meet the demands of modern life. Further, families that make that sort of investment in each other can reap the rewards of being rooted and being given the room to soar.

There are other connections with communal meals to be made as well. Consider the Margaret Atwood poem Bread. Its last line is, "Together, we eat this earth." A powerful cry to steward well the resources of the land, as well as a potent reminder of that line from the burial liturgy, "ashes to ashes, dust to dust."

Connecting the Generations

Think of the generational connections of communion. On First Communion Sunday, the extended family often shows up to witness their family member receive Christ's body and blood for the first time. What a natural day to talk about faith, to recall one's faith heritage, and to share faith stories, especially because those stories, passed on through the generations, shape families and change them, also. I think, for example, of the stories of perseverance that are part of Messiah's history. Their commitment to planting a congregation in Janesville, followed by their efforts to keep the doors open even in lean and uncertain times, and then ultimately to build a new facility, provides a window into the value of staying power, of stick-to-it-tive-ness that God and God's people have.

Our own individual faith stories are but a sliver of the larger story of the people of God who have been faithful throughout the centuries. This meal that Jesus instituted when he gathered with his closest friends connects us throughout all time with those who have gone before and those who are yet to come, to that great cloud of witnesses that Hebrews 12 talks about. No matter which Sunday First Communion is celebrated, it is critical that we remember this is not some "me and Jesus" moment. Instead, we join that throng of witnesses to whom the story of Jesus has been entrusted.

With that story also comes room: Room to forgive, room to trust, room to grow, room to reach, and room to welcome. I carry with me a vivid image from one of my first congregations. People gathered at the semi-circular, white and gold rail in a historic Norwegian church and knelt to receive the elements. As it happened, the table filled up, but not without leaving one person left standing alone. She would have been communing by herself (but not alone!) at the rail. As we started serving, a strange thing happened. People crowded to the left and to the right to make room for this dear soul. When she joined the group in the middle spot that had been cleared for her she said, "There's always room for one more at God's table." So, too, there is always room to share the gifts of the sacrament, including caring for others.

One might ask, "Don't these lessons apply to all congregations?" Yes, they do, but they may be more keenly felt in smaller congregations, whether they be rural or urban. In smaller congregations, the sense of connectedness runs deeper, and in smaller rural congregations, the family ties are often extended to the third and even fourth generation. More than once, I heard references to "our church family." The language fits. Like many families, churches of all sizes need to pay special attention to communication so that things run smoothly.

Chapter 6

Communicating Clearly

"Tell the members what they're doing; they might be surprised."
— Bob Gremmels

Another valuable component of congregational renewal stems from Messiah's approach to publications and public relations. No pastor could have had a better partner in this endeavor than I did. My husband's extensive background in church journalism and public relations, as well as his insistence on crafting quality publications, created a noticeably professional look that got people's attention. He also knew the power of telling a good story, of getting the word out using various formats, and of keeping people informed about all that the congregation was doing. That approach helped people see and learn about what the congregation was doing. Part of the focus was also on synodical events to help avoid the provincial mentality that can too easily set in. In some cases, for example, people were surprised by the depth and breadth of what the church did: missionary sponsorship, helping new mission start congregations, supporting social service agencies, and so on.

A polished look in publications is something I commend to all congregations. In this computer age, there is no reason to turn out anything less than quality material. If a church wants to be taken seriously, it helps to have publications that command respect and set the tone for ministry. Our newsletters had a consistent style, modeled in part after the format of "USA Today," where there was a lead story, an opinion section, briefs, and features all in pretty much the same space each month.

Newsletter

The monthly newsletter (The Messiah Messenger) was edited according to the AP style sheet and used correct grammar. Though that last item may sound pretty basic, it's essential for clear communications. Yes, not everyone has a trained church journalist to produce their publications, but there are plenty of grammar aids and helps available. An excellent resource is Fred Gonnerman's book Getting the Word Out, the Alban Guide to Church Communications (Alban Institute, 2003). Also invaluable is having someone else proofread your publications before going to press. After looking at the same basic words for so long, one's own eyes can glaze over, or correct the word, or simply gloss over the information without asking if it's accurate.

Another idea could involve strengthening the church and school connections by inviting the local high school journalism teacher and/or class to offer a critical eye and share some basic layout ideas. Once you have a layout that works for your purposes, stick with it. That way, people have a good idea of where to look for information if their reading time is limited. Using a consistent style comes with practice, but being consistent also sends a subtle message that one cares more about quality than trendiness.

It's Hard to be Crabby When...

Beyond stylistic considerations, though, was the public relations value of using one's newsletter to share the "good news stories" of the congregation. Telling those good news stories in as many venues as possible paid handsome dividends with those who struggled to believe things were turning around for Messiah. We discovered it was hard to be crabby when things were going well. Successes breed enthusiasm for mission and church leaders made sure the good things that were happening spread into homes and communities via the newsletter. The newsletter also became a teaching tool as it included tips for parenting, ideas for celebrating the seasons as families, and even on occasion, a recipe or two.

The Messenger was hardly a "puff piece" though. It conveyed the church council minutes, special reports as needed, and spoke to timely (and sometimes controversial) issues of the day. These items were addressed with an eye to the larger audience that would read them and thus were written up accordingly.

Bulletins

Quality regarding bulletins also matters. We tried various formats before settling on one that was user-friendly, had big-enough type, didn't waste a lot of paper, and was welcoming, inclusive, and instructive. We strived to avoid typos, more often successfully than not. Once, only a last-minute proofread saved the congregation from "passing the peach." Spell check wasn't that helpful when we typed out everything for the Christmas Eve bulletin, including the Nicene Creed. Our version initially read, "He has spoken through the profits." While that may have been true after the offering was received, we changed it to read "spoken through the prophets."

Brochures

Messiah's foray into quality publications extended to producing an outreach brochure. Shortly after my arrival, we assembled an introductory flyer. As the congregation grew, however, and wanted to extend its reach, we invested in a four-color brochure. It was a bold move. Color was not cheap, and we wanted these professionally produced. By this time we had lots of pictures from the various youth, family, and congregation events we'd hosted. Again, quality carried the day. We used short catchy phrases and interesting pictures to tell the story of Messiah.

Today, people can do many of their publications in-house, and many do a quality job because of the software and rising congregational expectations. This is good news, because too often churches have been willing to settle for something of a lesser quality. Such publications speak volumes about a church: Do we really believe giving God our best is something we're called to? In my various stints as a supply preacher in more than two dozen congregations in the synod, I've sometimes heard echoes of the sentiment, "Oh, we're just a little old country church. We don't need all those fancy things." Maybe not. But makeover congregations learn or discover the power of excellence to attract and generate interest.

A commitment to excellence also can mean not shying away from difficult topics. More than once, Messiah found itself trying to have conversations about various "hot button topics," subjects that generated passion along a wide spectrum of views. Such was the case with three particular topics: Sunday morning sports (addressed in chapter 3), stewardship and sexuality (addressed in Chapter 7). These topics are probably familiar in many congregations, and what may be a flashpoint for one church may not be so for another. The spiritual maturity of a congregation plays an important role in how various controversial subjects are both discussed and received. As Messiah confronted those issues, the congregation moved outside of its comfort zone on more than one occasion, and it also learned that there was a price to be paid for some of the decisions it made.

Media Today

Today, of course, many congregations are using a host of technological tools to share the good news and to get out word about their ministries. As one who doesn't adapt easily to new technology, it took me a while to come around to some of the usages for technology in ministry. Now, with that confession on the table, I have to say that I've grown in my appreciation for and awareness of what technology can do to help congregations and institutions. I also feel more competent than I did initially, so while I may never be on the cutting edge of using the "next thing," using the tools of technology for ministry has added yet more tools to the ministry tool box. And isn't that part of the call? Figuring out ways to connect with those whom we've been called to serve?

In my neck of the woods, the northeastern section of Iowa, congregations are using social media in various ways: announcing events and celebrations, creating prayer-request links, posting pictures of mission work, having on-line Bible studies, promoting stewardship awareness through Twitter chats, giving shout-outs to people and projects, sharing newsletters and upcoming events.

The Northeastern Iowa Synod also has a Director of Evangelical Mission, Reverend Joelle Colville-Hanson, whose usage of technology has helped further connect congregations and has extended the reach of ministry. She has created a synod-wide bulletin board for any of our congregations to advertise their events on. By combining her photography with scripture and/or hymnody, Reverend Colville-Hanson also creates a daily devotional that reflects the beauty of the area. Additionally, there is "God's Work, Our Blog," a regular blog about current events and stewardship information.

She also edits the weekly "Strengthening the Church" synod blog that informs congregations of events, notifies readers of what the synod staff is up to, keeps people informed of current events, connects readers to the national church, and serves as a prayer and mission bulletin board.

Some of the same basic journalistic principles that cover written publications can inform web-based and social media: current, relevant, and accurate information matter. Good social media manners matter, too, because our churches are being represented and, by extension, God.

In chapter 2 of her book The Social Media Gospel, author Meredith Gould connects theology and faith to allow social media users to mirror through their media the basic framework of their belief system: belief in a gracious God, for instance, can help generate a gracious media presence for online interactions (Kindle Loc. 336).

Online giving is also another use for web-based ministry that some congregations are engaging in. This is an attractive option for those who wish to support their church but are not able to be there all the time. Making ministry accessible, with clear lines of communication in multiple formats that create avenues of connectivity, helps our people know that we value them and are willing to be flexible when it comes to how we can serve them.

Chapter 7

Outside the Comfort Zones: Stewardship and other Lessons

"Stewardship is everything we do after we say 'I believe'."
— Clarence Stoughton, quoted from Northeastern Iowa Stewardship website

Few things in congregational ministry are as challenging as creating a healthy understanding of stewardship. It's safe to say that this is an area where the real-life encounter with giving to God I experienced at Janesville changed me; I had a makeover of my own understanding of stewardship that classroom learning couldn't really teach. The broad category of stewardship often gets attention in the fall of the year, when many congregations crank up their annual giving programs. This yearly ritual often causes anxiety for preacher and people alike, as pastors try to figure out yet another way of helping people see how amazingly blessed they are to be able to respond generously to God's goodness and as parishioners brace for what some perceive will be a harangue about giving.

I can appreciate both sentiments. An experience from my twenties still causes me to smile. When I was new to a community in my post-college days, I visited a couple of area churches before deciding which one to join. Church A was a big, established historical church. Church B hadn't been around as long and was smaller and less formal. On both Sundays that I visited church A, the preacher talked about money. The preacher in church B did not preach about money, so I joined church B. I am thankful that my understanding of stewardship since then has grown exponentially. Ironically, after I was married, I joined my husband's church: Church A.

Transformation Gets Personal

My growth in understanding stewardship came as a direct result of my ministry at Messiah. Talk about transformation! My spouse and I realized early on that our own personal stewardship would be a statement of our belief in what God was doing in our midst and in the congregation. We became generous givers. It was amazing. God really did — and does — take care of us. After hearing about this approach for a long time, but never really being challenged to publicly live it out, we began to discover the joy of putting God first with our offerings. What made the difference was that we modeled the abundance of God. So often congregations, especially those who have had a run of bad luck, pastorates that don't click, or other woes, start to see only their deficits — what they don't have. It is a recipe for cheapness — for just getting by. There indeed may be times when we all need to do some belt-tightening, but being cheap with and toward God is never the place to start.

In fact, living out of an abundance model creates gratitude and generosity; abundance giving inspires others to see how blessed they are, too. When we told the good folks at Messiah, for example, that we intended to commit the equivalent of one year of my salary to our four-year capital campaign, that set the tone. I can still see the astonished face of one parishioner who understood what that kind of belief in a downtrodden congregation meant.

Some said, "You're lucky you can do that." Not really. We overextended ourselves but somehow God made it work. That's the key. God makes it work. God is always willing to match our enthusiasm! There isn't a person reading these words who couldn't similarly step out more boldly in faith somehow (financial or otherwise). It's the difference between merely giving and truly investing ourselves in building God's church.

But beware: Abundance giving isn't an easy sell for many of us who like our creature comforts. It may not go over well when the preacher invites people to look at themselves in the mirror and asks them to take stock of the various toys, gadgets, and transportation equipment they have. I learned that lesson the hard way. After I'd been at the congregation for a number of years, at a time when costs were rising and dollars shrinking, I said in a meeting with the church council, after pointing out the window to the vehicles in the parking lot, "We don't have a have financial problem, we have a spiritual problem." Ouch. It may have been a true statement, but it sounded heavy-handed. I should have used the journalistic questioning approach and asked something like "Is this a financial problem? Or Is this a spiritual problem?" and then let the questions hang in the air. To this day, I try to remember to use a gentler approach; spiritual smugness isn't pretty.

Loanership, Losses, Great Gain

The truth of the matter is that many North American Christians do have a spiritual problem when it comes to giving. We think the money is ours to do with as we like. We are people who have forgotten loanership. All we have is on loan to us from God.

That philosophy also means that I, too, have to examine my purchases and acquisitions through the same lens. What am I doing with the stuff I accumulate? In 1999, we experienced a flood in Waverly. (In 2008, we experienced an even more devastating flood, but that's another story.) My husband's older daughter called us late in the evening while we were on vacation in central Minnesota and told us the rains were heavy and the rivers rising. That night, we hastily packed our suitcases, tried to get a few hours of sleep, and then headed home early the next day. Upon arrival, we saw the sandbag crew set up in our driveway. The neighborhood was pitching in and soon, a sandbag snake stretched up and down the backyards of our block.

An evacuation order had already been given, but we had time to bring things out of the basement to what we hoped would be the safety of the first floor. What we couldn't haul up, we put up higher in the basement. We were prepared for four feet of water. The last thing my husband did was to open the casement windows downstairs so the water could come in and equalize the pressure. When we were allowed back in our house three days later, we discovered that we'd had five feet of river water in the house. It left a coating of black sludge everywhere. Latex paint on sheet-rocked walls bulged out; plastic buckets of toys were floating in the stairwell. We lost a lot of stuff in that flood. We later joked that it was a great way to get a clean basement because we had to strip everything down to the studs.

Yet the blessings of that time far outweighed any stuff we had to pitch. We were sheltered for those three days by my husband's daughter, who immediately called and opened her home to us. When the clean-up began, at least a dozen members of the congregation came to assist, and I'm convinced there's a special spot in heaven for people who haul out soggy sheet rock. The Red Cross came and fed us, the neighborhood, and all the volunteers for a week or so. Ravioli, peas, and pears never tasted so good. One day, a woman I didn't recognize drove up, stopped her vehicle, got out of the car, and gave us a huge two-pack of bleach. She did the same for many others in the area, I later learned. We joked then that the smell in our area was "Eau du Chlorine." Yes, we lost a lot of stuff, and I very humanly lamented the loss of some irreplaceable Christmas ornaments collected for decades, but the blessings of that time are innumerable.

Time for a Heart Check

When our possessions get in the way of responding generously to God's goodness, it's time to re-examine our own hearts. Part of a pastor's call is to help people perform regular spiritual heart-check-ups, allowing them to assess their relationship with God.

A stewardship heart-check can be bold and direct, but it has to include things like worship and prayer, Bible study and service, participation and education. Abundance giving can be tricky, though, sort of like a two-edged sword: How much we give isn't a direct indication of our relationship with God, yet giving abundantly reflects our gratitude toward God and our awareness that God is the source of all. God will never fault us for being rich toward God with our time, our talent, or our treasure.

It's also time to re-examine our own hearts when we think we're "paying too much" for ministry. I've encountered that as well. Some congregations have what I'll call "purse watchers," people whose purpose can often appear to be ensuring that the budget is tight, the preacher knows his or her place, and there's very little room for benevolence. It saddens me when I encounter this. It's even sadder when that attitude is part of congregational leadership. So much joy is squeezed out as every penny is watched and the movement toward transformation can be thwarted. Congregations begin living out of a scarcity model rather than abundance model. Is this really the kind of approach to money God wants? The rich young ruler in Mark 10 went away sorrowful because he couldn't part with his stuff to help others. How sorrowful those other hearts must be who cannot see the bigger vision God's generosity makes possible through our own generous responses.

As someone engaged in transformational ministry, one of my true joys has been helping congregations let light and air into their midst. Some of that process has involved increasing budgets for the sake of mission and outreach, connecting people with organizations and agencies that benefit from their dollars and using the offerings of the people to create a sense of welcome and care.

At Messiah, the capital campaign preparation work opened our eyes to how we could increase our giving. Working with an outside consultant, the congregation was challenged to increase its giving to roughly 2.3% of income for the area. The capital campaign was successful, and the congregation was able to move forward with building. Once we had a mortgage for the new facility, we also had something very tangible to give toward. It helped that the conversations about the cost of the facility were similar to those people have when buying a house. People in the area were taking out similar size loans for one-family dwellings. With the church, we had lots of families willing to contribute to cover the mortgage. The capital campaign helped us get realistic in our giving, encouraged us to increase our offerings accordingly, and kept us honest in giving to God.

It goes without saying that in order to be healthy, congregations benefit from being externally focused. Congregations often get in trouble when they focus solely on their concerns, their needs, their wishes. This is not necessarily an immediate concern in makeover churches, but people still need to be aware that such narcissism leads to selfishness; such self-centeredness leads to internal collapse and often thwarts the mission of the gospel. For congregations in the midst of ministry renewal, finding ways to reach beyond themselves is vital to becoming healthy. At Messiah, we came out of our shell in various ways. We became a member congregation of the local Lutheran retirement community. We sent quilts to our local Bible camp for their fall festival. We used our facility to host various community events.

In other words, part of our transformation involved being both good stewards of our property as well as being good stewards of the resources entrusted to us. In concrete ways, we learned and lived out the notion that we could make a difference, both where we were planted and in the larger contexts to which we were connected by our partnership with the ELCA and its institutions.

More Learning

One of the real blessings of a transformational site is the energy newcomers generate.

We were blessed with people who weren't afraid of getting involved even though they'd been at the church only a short time. For some of the faithful long-term members, having others willing to pitch in meant those who had kept the church going in the lean times could take a breather if they needed to.

Despite the rush of energy that new members can bring, and the desire we had to build up the church, I sometimes wish we had taken even more time to let potential members acclimate to the congregation before encouraging membership. People join a church for all sorts of reasons: wanting a church wedding for their offspring, reacting to concerns at another congregation, wanting their young children involved in Sunday school and confirmation, and the list goes on.

Sometimes, people who join in haste haven't worked through their own reasons sufficiently, and when something flares up that they don't like, or when the reason they came has been met, they leave, become inactive, or they grouse and grumble. If they stay and get involved behind the scenes, they see that their new church has its troubles, too, and they see that it may not be the idyllic institution they expected. People are sometimes surprised — and then disillusioned — to find that the new church is a very human institution and has its share of politics, bickering, and private kingdom building. There is no such thing as a perfect church.

Giving people time to acclimate, to see the congregation through the ups and downs and the rhythms of the year, allows them to see some of the human frailties and hopefully helps them realize that the church isn't a museum of saints, but is made up of flesh-and-blood people like themselves, trying to be the body of Christ in a broken and hurting world, who can do extraordinary things, but who also can blow it on occasion, too. What binds us together in a transformational setting or anywhere else, is the baptismal promise that daily we rise to new life, and we can begin again as loved, forgiven, and claimed people.

Discovering Your Strengths

Another helpful lesson for transformational ministry flows from the book Now, Discover Your Strengths. The authors, Marcus Buckingham and Donald Clifton, advocate for an asset-based approach to life, career, hobbies, job searches, and encourage readers to build on their strengths rather than trying to compensate for one's weaknesses. The idea makes sense. Congregations sometimes feel pressure to be all things to all people. That's fine, especially if one belongs to a large church with multiple layers of staffing, but many congregations are far from that size. So, ask yourself, "What does my congregation do really well? How can we build on those strengths?" Determine what your strengths are: Family ministry? Innovative worship? Meals? Hospitality? Fighting poverty? Global missions? Senior ministry? Lead from your strengths, the book encourages.

In another handy guide, The Great Permission, An Asset-Based Field Guide for Congregations, author Bob Sitze uses ten illuminating case studies to help congregations size up their mission and ministry potential. The sidebar sections "Another Look" nicely encapsulate the ideas offered in each "How To" section.

Both books encourage readers to be willing to look, also, at those areas where maybe you don't need to focus as much energy or allocate as many resources so that people can shift and utilize resources according to their strengths. In a transformational setting, this approach can help alleviate the temptation for a church to become overly pastor-centered. Yes, the pastor provides leadership and helps chart direction, but a lot of that comes from listening first and acting second. One of the things I learned along the way was to tuck away in my mind's eye the talents people offered up during the course of conversation.

We relied on those skills and abilities as we plugged people into various needs that arose: asking a woodworker to make wooden candle holders for a Christmas program; asking the quilting group to make quilts for our seniors and asking someone else to embroider the squares; recruiting various craftspeople to contribute items for the fundraising auction for the youth group mission trips; utilizing the owner of a print shop for our newsletters and posters for the various displays; drafting the journalism professor to write professional press releases, to create ad copy for the paper, and to produce a first-rate church newsletter.

These may sound basic to many readers, and many congregations already do these things, but for us, realizing the assets we had in our midst propelled us into new areas of ministry that generated interest and enthusiasm and brought our mission to life. We could still remember when the future looked less than hopeful, so capitalizing on our assets filled us with possibility and renewed us.

Had Messiah received its $50,000 gift at a different time in our life, we might have engaged in equipping people earlier. But without the building, the space it afforded, the energy it engendered, and the renewal it prompted in all areas of our life together, we were somewhat limited. And while we were in the old building, we did what many of us did when we were growing up: We did what we could with what we had. But the new facility generated momentum for mission that we hadn't quite visualized.

Risking for the Gospel

Ministry is often about stepping out in faith and taking risks. Our willingness to risk for the gospel in a way we couldn't have initially imagined came into being when I was approached by a pastor from an area congregation. She had an even smaller congregation than we did, no youth program, and her future was uncertain at the congregation due to budget concerns. She was also a non-partnered lesbian.

Over coffee, she and I discussed the possibilities for sharing some ministry areas. Her church had strong male Bible study leaders; we had talked about starting a men's Bible study program, "Guys Talking to Guys About God." She had a few youth who would benefit from connecting with other kids; we had a youth person on staff.

"Could our congregations look at working together on some of these things?" she asked. I took the idea to our church council and got everything on the table. We formed a joint task force with her congregation to explore the possibilities. We each met with our respective bishops to hash things over. We hosted a congregational meeting to discuss the idea. There were heated opinions, but the congregation agreed to try the arrangement for one year for the sake of the youth. And we did. The men's Bible study met weekly with a group of six to eight men, with roughly half from each church. Youth programming never really took off, though the joint family canoe trip and potluck was successful. A few families left the congregation because of their strong anti-gay clergy sentiments. The rumblings and grumblings began. Even so, the church council and the task force continued to believe that moving outside comfort zones could ultimately be a powerful witness to the gospel.

I wish I could say all went well after that. It didn't. In our age of comfort and convenience, we sometimes forget that pain can be part of the Christian learning curve. As a congregation, we were about to discover how steep that learning curve could get. The day came when the pastor of the other church stopped by to visit. She told me she was in love. She had found a life partner and was going to have her union blessed in the coming year. While I rejoiced at her love, I grieved for the loss we were about to encounter.

Knowing where many of the congregations in the ELCA were, and where my own synod was at that time, I suspected the other pastor's partnership meant the end of the shared congregational relationship was on the horizon, so I met with my bishop. The church council at Messiah met. The pastor and I engaged in dialogue as to what her decision meant. We terminated the relationship between our congregations, thankful for what we had attempted, yet saddened that the partnership we had entered into was undone by an unforeseen partnership of a different sort.

Had our congregation been engaged in sexuality conversations for many years, like some congregations, things might have gone differently. Had I believed it necessary for our congregation to take a stronger positive stand on this issue, things might have gone differently. Had I been more clear in my own reactions at the time, things might have gone differently. And had I been willing to risk splitting Messiah over this issue, I might have pressed harder, argued more forcefully, staked more of myself on this issue. But I didn't. Maybe it's justification by rationalization, but given the climate in rural northeastern Iowa in 2003-2004, I remain grateful that we were willing to risk for the gospel in our small congregation. Who knows what God's Spirit will accomplish one day because we were willing to let in a little light and air?

Congregational Stamina

Finally, we also learned to pay attention to congregational stamina. As the building project neared completion and we geared up for our September Dedication Sunday, we realized we were tired. Energy expended on physical labor such as landscaping and interior prep work, combined with the mental energy required by dedication details, plus the ongoing work for fall programming, filled our plates. Not to mention all that had transpired previously with the capital campaign, the building details themselves, and the daily tasks of ministry and mission.

We took some time and delayed the start of most of our fall programming. Could we have done more along the way to build in some down time? Perhaps. But we wanted to get this building done! For our charter members, the wait had been 43 years.

What else would I have done differently? I would have made a special effort to train people for ministry tasks earlier; they were already doing ministry well before I showed up. But there was room to grow and learn, and we eventually got there. The way things happened with the building gift, though, meant that a capital campaign, land acquisition, architectural details, building permits, and the thousand other details that accompany getting a building erected, became our primary focus.

When the time came to explore a sabbatical, seven years into my call, the congregation was ready to take that next step. We took a year to get ready, so that after eight years together, I was granted a three-month sabbatical. (More on that in chapter 9.) This planned time away afforded a great opportunity to invite people in more deeply to congregational leadership, and I'm thankful we did that, but it might have been beneficial to intentionally "equip the saints" earlier. On the other hand, it takes a pastor a while to figure out the dynamics of a parish, to earn the community's trust, to occasionally work through issues related to the previous pastorates, to discern the congregational resources and the community needs, so rushing in to take over is rarely the best course of action.

Chapter 8

The Song Is Right, but There's More to it Than That

"The church is not a building, a committee, or a board..."
— Jay Beech, The Church Song

By now, some readers may be asking, "Couldn't we have engaged in all this transformational ministry in the old building? Couldn't we have become a makeover church without a new facility?" After all, the Jay Beech song, quoted above, is right, but there is another question to attend as well, "Does building drive mission or does mission drive building?" For some, that may be a "chicken and egg" question.

For Messiah, it became obvious that our mission not only drove our new facility but opened us to new possibilities for mission, too. As surely as our old facility hindered much of our mission because of its inaccessibility, its size, and its lack of aesthetics, the new facility created opportunities for mission and became a terrific tool. The church became a community resource in ways that wouldn't have been possible previously. For one thing, the new facility was accessible — all on one floor, at driveway level. There was no going down uneven outside stairs or steep interior ones to get into the basement. The facility was also beautiful, with open spaces and good lighting both day and night.

More than that, though, was a sense of pride the new building generated. The men now took turns hosting the monthly fellowship breakfast that before had been held only at the Methodist church in town. The women met weekly for quilting year-round because there was space for set-up as well as storage. The youth hosted lock-ins and other events because there was ample room to maneuver, play games, watch videos, do crafts, or simply unwind.

The church's proximity to the school (two blocks away) benefitted the community. The church hosted the Homecoming pre-game meal for the football players. When there was a scheduling mix-up with another facility and the local "Teens Against Tobacco Use" needed a sizable space for the area school groups to meet, they called the church and brought the meeting there on short notice. The Red Cross designated the church a safe evacuation site for emergencies.

On a Bigger Stage

Beyond the community, Messiah was recognized in a way few could have anticipated when we began our ministry together in June, 1996. The Evangelical Lutheran Church in America's (ELCA) Division for Outreach sponsored a workshop in 2003 called "Come, See, Discover Ministry in Action." Messiah, chosen as the Region 5 site, began organizing for the event. The goal was to provide "in-depth looks at mission and ministry directed to unchurched and marginalized communities."

The Reverend Frederick Mason, Division for Outreach staff, said, "The program hopes to provide interested participants with an experience that can clarify connections between vocational choices and opportunities in mission development ministry."

To go from being a congregation whose future was bleak to being one selected to host an event sponsored by the national church thrilled us. When Messiah was chosen as a "Come, See, Discover" (CSD) workshop site, we were humbled and elated, not to mention just a bit overwhelmed by what the event might entail: Housing, transportation, meals, programs, materials — all became separate committees headed by various volunteers.

Deciding how to best utilize the day, we settled on a rotation format and established conversation stations that we utilized after an opening large-group presentation. The synod and area institutions partnered with us. The Northeastern Iowa Synod is blessed with an abundance of ELCA-related places. Waverly itself, just five miles north of Messiah, is home to Wartburg College, Bartels Lutheran Retirement Community, Lutheran Services in Iowa-Bremwood campus, and to the synod office. Seven miles south, in Cedar Falls, is the Lutheran Student Center on the University of Northern Iowa campus. These agencies shared various promotional items for the hospitality packet each CSD participant received.

When the big day arrived, guests were welcomed with the warmth characteristic of Messiah. Following welcome and registration, participants gathered in the sanctuary for a large-group presentation. We were fortunate to have some charter members of the congregation still living. They were first-hand witnesses to the congregation's history and gladly shared their memories and stories. Some had laid brick, painted walls, paid the mortgage, helped build the original structure, and stayed the course during the difficult days. For them, the event proved emotional and rewarding.

Part of what made the day meaningful included sharing the "scripture pegs" that undergirded much of the ministry at Messiah. Jeremiah 29:11 repeatedly reminded us that God had a future and a hope for us. For a congregation that had weathered various disappointments this passage was good news! Equally heartening were the words from Second Corinthians 5: In Christ, we are new creations; the old has passed away, see, everything has become new. These permission-giving verses encouraged the congregation and the pastor to step boldly into the future God was still creating, to live into the new life that God was bringing forth.

Holy Jumper Cables?

As the transformation continued, it occurred to me that a great image for what Messiah was experiencing was similar to what happens when jumper cables are used to jump-start a car. Why? Think about how jumper cables work: The battery you're jumping may only be "playing possum" and may not be truly dead. Usually, there's enough life left in the battery that the jumper cables, when connected to another life-giving source, get the juice flowing again in the flagging battery and bring that battery back to life. So, too, with many congregations. There's life there, but you may have to work a bit to get mission and ministry jump-started. The jump-start you need can come from a variety and combination of sources: God, the belief others have in your mission, your own congregation, yourself. Leaders in congregations need to believe in what God is making possible. The pastor and key leaders need to catch hold of the vision and then keep that vision before people, especially when the future may seem darker rather than brighter.

Instructive, also, to the task of becoming a makeover congregation is a clip from the Disney movie The Princess Diaries. That clip is especially helpful for congregations whose inner beauty may have become hidden, who may be struggling to be transformed. The film itself chronicles the transformation of a gawky teenager into a true princess. In the "Mia Makeover" scene at the hands of the hairdresser, the "fabulous Paolo," audiences watch Mia lose her frizzy hair, her bushy eyebrows, and her geeky glasses. What emerges is the hidden beauty of the princess in training. Lessons gleaned for congregations include these:

1. Be willing to take a closer look. Underneath Mia's bushy eyebrows and frizzy hair was a beautiful young woman waiting to emerge, but it took a willingness to look more closely to see her beauty. The same is true for congregations; sometimes what's beautiful about congregations has been hidden because of frustration or neglect or pastors who behave in ways that discourage congregations from shining and sharing their gifts.
2. "Let the work begin," the queen tells Paolo as the makeover begins for Mia, her granddaughter. Similarly, congregations need to be willing to work for the beautiful instead of settling for average. A pastoral commitment to excellence can be a powerful model in this regard.
3. Have the right tools. In the movie, Paolo used his tools of blow dryer and curling iron for the transformation. God uses the tools of grace, hope, forgiveness, hard work, mercy, and possibility to create makeover options. Congregations and pastors willing to utilize those same tools will find themselves moving nicely into the future God is creating.

4. Watch out for distractions that can get in the way. For Paolo, that meant removing his rings. In our congregations, the extraneous items can include the powers of evil that are more than happy to try to get in the way as congregations get healthier. But remember: God is always stronger than evil.
5. Be willing to break a few things. In the movie, it was a hairbrush and eyeglasses. We don't need that kind of tit-for-tat, but we do need to break old patterns and discover new possibilities. How to do that? Listen first, ask lots of questions, take the time to educate people about options, and then wade in gently with making changes.
6. Bring in outside help if necessary. Even though Paolo was laughable and arrogant, he helps us see that sometimes we need to bring in others to help turn things around. Ask people to help; keep track of their talents and abilities, and then put those resources to good use. People may not respond to a "cattle call" for help, but if they know you're asking them to help because of a specific talent or ability they have, the likelihood of their involvement increases.

Time and Effort

Unless one consults with an expert, good facial makeovers rarely happen quickly. Often, a person has to experiment with different products and shades to see what really works for them. Carmindy, of the TLC show "What Not to Wear," made most any makeover look simple. While I enjoy the fact that she went for the "less is more" theory, I know it still takes some people a long time to figure out what works. Count me in that category. Usually, to my daughter's chagrin, I just fall back on the standard of a little blush and some simple mascara.

Likewise, congregations often have to take a while to figure out what works and what doesn't work for them. The fear of something not working shouldn't prevent folks from trying something new and/or different. If something doesn't work, we can still learn from it. At our house, some attempts that go awry are jokingly labeled "science experiments."

With makeovers, be they personal or congregational, someplace along the way, many seem to stand at the precipice deciding whether to stick with the standards or to be bold and creative; deciding whether or not to step out into faith; deciding whether to move forward or to retrench; deciding that sometimes, transformation also involves the proverbial "two steps forward, one step back," at least for a while, until transformation truly takes hold.

Leaping from the Lion's Head

The great scene toward the end of the movie *Indiana Jones and the Last Crusade* helps illustrate the crucible that some congregations find themselves in. In the movie, Jones has to step out in faith from the lion's head, trusting that there will be a bridge to carry him across a chasm. All looks bleak; it's a long way to the bottom of the crevasse. Jones has been told that only those who believe will be able to continue the quest. How true for congregations! And daunting as well. Daunting because it can be a scary thing to move into God's new creation. At Messiah, part of our stepping out in faith meant new faces and new voices in leadership positions, increased expectations, greater commitments, a higher profile, more active outreach, stronger stewardship, expanded programming, and a host of other possibilities not quite imagined when the journey together first started. In our stepping out, God stepped out with us, too, and God made the makeover work.

Chapter 9

Looking to the Future

"I offer a toast. The undiscovered country... the future."
— Chancellor Gorkon,
Star Trek VI: The Undiscovered Country

After the push of fundraising, blueprints, building, dedication, and emerging ministries made possible by the new facility — as well as the ongoing tasks of daily ministry — it was time for a pause. We'd worked hard from 1996-2003 to build a new church for a new century, to build the mission and ministry, to become a community resource. Stepping out of ministry for a while seemed a good thing, for both pastor and parish. One such way of stepping out is to take a sabbatical. Sabbaticals provide an extended time of leave away from the parish and are designed to foster renewal. They were coming into vogue in my synod. A few years earlier, I had witnessed the renewal my mentor enjoyed when he had taken a sabbatical. After mulling the idea over a while, I decided to explore one.

The plan was to be gone for three months. Well before that time arrived, though, I visited with the church council to propose the idea, roughly a full year ahead of when I'd hoped to be on sabbatical. Later, the council president and I presented the particulars to the congregation at the annual meeting. Advance planning laid the groundwork for a time away and allowed the congregation time to get on board with the idea of the pastor being gone for a twelve-week study and renewal leave.

The old adage, "When the cat's away, the mice will play" is a far cry from what happened when we actually embarked on the sabbatical. In the time that elapsed between floating the idea with the council, presenting it to the congregation for approval, and my actual departure, roughly a year later, the council and I laid out the program so that people in the congregation could find ways to engage with the ministry needs that would exist while I was gone.

Worship leadership was a primary concern. We lined up guest preachers for communion Sundays. For the other Sundays, we trained lay leadership worship teams of three to four people who were responsible for lessons, children's messages, sermons, and liturgies. I met with them, gave them worship resources and lots of encouragement. Together, we fleshed out a rough overview for their assigned Sunday.

Pastoral care coverage afforded us an opportunity for cooperation, too, as the local Methodist pastor agreed to help with hospital visits. Fellow Lutheran clergy agreed to be on stand-by for funerals. Home-care callers were trained to visit the shut-ins and bring the sacrament to them. Since the sabbatical ran from early May to early August, the education program was winding down, and there were good people in place to wrap up the year.

Three-pronged Sabbatical

I had a three-pronged approach for what I planned to do during sabbatical. Contemporary services were growing in popularity, so I wanted to investigate those. My family and I traveled to a number of area churches in the Midwest and explored what we might bring back to Messiah.

Another prong was the rest and renewal component; for me, dirt therapy (gardening) figured prominently in my plans. The hosta beds in my yard now attest to my zealous gardening in the summer of 2004. Renewal through reading was also part of the agenda.

The third prong was to spend time with my family, away, which we did. We were given the use of a cabin in Ely, Minnesota, home to the Boundary Waters Canoe Area. We planned to enjoy a week in Milwaukee, taking in a Global Mission Event, among other things. We also scheduled in a week-long event at Luther College called Lutherlag, which is basically an "Elderhostel for Families," and provided opportunities for continuing education as well as renewal through the arts.

Finally, the plans and permissions were in place. The time to leave was at hand. After investing so much of myself in this congregation, and after all they'd given my family, would I be able to step away? Really step away? I was about to find out.

The first month was the hardest. I was so used to being busy that I felt I had to do something almost all the time. It's a good thing that during that first month our daughter was in school, or she probably would have been pressed into staying busy, too. Eventually, I learned to unwind. I went for walks along the river. I sat outside and read. I napped. I worked on a quilt or two.

I also kept the learning components of sabbatical in front of me. Having a chance to explore other congregations and their worship styles was educational. The churches we visited didn't venture too far afield from typical Lutheran service order. Differences were mainly noted in music choices and instrumentation. Churches that had paid music staff people had a bit more variety. The overall atmosphere of those contemporary services was more relaxed, but since Messiah already had a pretty relaxed approach to worship, this particular aspect of contemporary worship wasn't something the congregation needed specifically to work on.

Benefits of the sabbatical were numerous for pastor and parish. I returned with a renewed sense of energy and ideas. And, indicative of how far the congregation had come and how healthy they had become, people realized their church could flourish despite an extended pastoral absence. The sense of ownership engendered by my leave also fostered a deeper awareness of the demands and tasks of pastoral ministry.

I heard about a particularly delightful event only upon my return. One of our transformation steps involved increasing our benevolence and we chose to help sponsor a missionary. We helped support the work of Eliseo and Regina Perez, who were stationed in Puerto Rico. While on leave they visited some of the congregations that had sponsored them, including Messiah. In July, 2004, the congregation sans pastor hosted the missionary couple. All went well, and the congregation and our missionaries enjoyed some great food, fellowship and accommodations — another example of the hospitality that marks Messiah. They spent time together learning about the work and ministry of "our missionaries," sharing stories and asking questions, and thus strengthened the international ties of the church and its people. The people took care of the hosting and worship details in fine form. It was a memorable time for all involved.

My question at the beginning — Could I really get away? — was answered. Sabbatical taught me that yes, I could leave, which was something I hadn't known until part-way through the pastoral pause afforded by a sabbatical. We'd accepted the call to Messiah when our daughter was seven months old. My husband used to wheel her into the church in her stroller and park her in the back. This congregation watched her grow from baby to toddler to young lady. They laughed at her antics and showered her with affection. She grew up knowing church as a warm, welcoming, wonderful place where she was valued, loved, and encouraged. That love and affection was one of the deep ties we had to Messiah. It was strange to be away from that for three months. It was good to be away, but it was also good to come back.

Yet coming back was different, too. It wasn't exactly a case of picking up where we'd left off. The congregation had grown in confidence and awareness of the demands of ministry. But some never really understood how a pastor could take a three-month break and still retain her job, and so there was a bit of upset about that. Some who'd helped out were also weary and more than willing to hand back the pastoral tasks they'd taken on. A period of adjustment ensued as people sorted out their concerns and voiced them. Together, the congregation and pastor made the transition back into shared ministry and fall programming got underway. But I'd been changed by the sabbatical. So had the congregation.

Chapter 10

Leaving Well

You've got to know when to hold 'em; know when to fold 'em.
— Kenny Rogers, "The Gambler"

Knowing when to leave a congregation is a balancing act unlike few others. Stay too long, despite regular vacation, continuing education and days off, and one risks stagnation. Leave too soon and one rarely experiences the deep connectedness that can make for healthy, vital, and vibrant ministry.

In his November 27, 2009, column, USA Today founder Al Neuharth commended celebrity Oprah Winfrey for her decision to quit her TV show while she was still going strong. Neuharth said, "She's quitting while she's still ahead." Neuharth later stated, "She should be an example for many hangers-on who don't know when to hang it up," and he termed this condition "hangonitis."

After more than nine years at MLC, my husband, Bob, and I started to explore the issue of leaving. Our daughter was moving into those critical pre-teen years; Bob had experienced some health issues that had gotten our attention, and there was a general feeling that perhaps it was time to step aside. We prayed and pondered our decision for months. Two events tipped the scales in favor of coming home.

One was a fall Bob had in August when I was at a church event and our daughter, then eight, called and in tears said, "Papa fell, and he's bleeding. Can you come home?" Not knowing how injured Bob was, I talked to him briefly and discovered his injuries weren't life-threatening though he was bleeding, and the entryway where he had fallen was a mess. Quickly, I told the chair of our event what had happened and that I had to leave. Racing those five miles home, I continued to hear the upset in my daughter's voice. When I got home, Bob was sitting in a chair, tending his injuries, and our daughter had cleaned up the bloody entryway.

The second event that tipped the scales came a few months later, during a hectic autumn. Since I was in a part-time call, I had tried hard to not be gone more than three nights at most during the week. This particular week, though, I had to be gone four nights in a row. When I told our daughter about being gone yet again, and thereby missing bedtime prayers and snuggles, she said, "Another meeting?" and broke out in tears. In my head, I heard myself say, "I can do something about this." And so I did. We set in motion the mechanics for leaving.

While we were praying and pondering, my husband and I had also been examining our finances to see if I could afford to be home for a while. In the end, we decided that I could be home. The decision to resign having been made, we now considered how to tell the congregation. Consulting with a mentor, the synod staff, and my family, I took the "short and sweet" approach to leaving. Drawing out our departure would only generate more pain, so we announced our decision to leave first to the church council and then to the congregation the following Sunday. Three weeks later, we were gone. It was a short time table, I'll admit, and others in other situations may choose differently, or their governing bodies may require more notice be given, but in this situation, not belaboring the good-bye was important. I thanked the congregation for the privilege of having served as their pastor, asked forgiveness for the mistakes I'd made, offered the same to them, and commended them to God's care and keeping. We were given a lovely send-off, and the congregation was gracious to our family. We were thankful for what we had accomplished together. But the time to leave had come; the congregation was about to write another chapter in its life, as were we in our family's life. The future beckoned.

Because we lived only five miles from the congregation, we knew we had to make a clean and firm break for the health of the congregation and our own well-being. Often, pastors don't fully let go when they leave. As the conference dean for ten years, I heard too many stories of pastors interfering with former congregations.

I refused to join that group. So let go we did, but not without cost. Saying good-bye to people one loves is rarely simple, and the temptation to hang on is intense. But one has to be willing to let go in order for the ministry to move forward, for the congregation to move in different directions, and for the Spirit to work.

When the final Sunday came, we had a very public service of farewell and departure. During the service, I gave the congregation president the keys to the office. I announced to all there that morning that I would not be able to come back to serve in a pastoral capacity. Even so, as I drove back and forth those last weeks, I also practiced in the car the speech that I knew I would invariably have to make when someone called to ask me if I could come back for a funeral or a wedding. Sure enough, a few months after I left, someone called and asked if I could do the service for their mother. She'd been a shut-in, and I had shared communion, consolation, and conversation with her during the 9 plus years I was at Messiah. So I said basically the speech that I'd worked up. It went something like, "That's very kind of you to ask, but I'm sorry, I really can't come back to do that. Thank you so much for thinking of me, though. Might I recommend...." And then the conversation wrapped up. Even years after I had been gone — in one case five years; in another, nine the phone calls came. And I had to say the same thing. As difficult as it was to say the words, I knew they were the right ones to say. There is a certain heartbreak and loneliness in ministry, and times like those phone calls reinforce that. But they also point to the necessity of having healthy boundaries all along in one's ministry.

In the midst of the discernment process regarding departure, I realized that I'd taken the congregation as far as it was willing to go at that time in its life. Stepping aside well — graciously and firmly — allowed the congregation to explore what other daring things God might be calling it to. Now, I belong to the congregation's past, but the transformations God effected when the journey toward becoming a makeover congregation began are on-going.

God is at work in your congregation, too. What challenges do you face? What scripture pegs do you hang your ministry on? Where do you want to let in light and air? What hidden beauty does your congregation have? These are but a few of the questions you can explore as you look through the makeover tool kits at the end of this book. Each kit is designed to lead your congregation on an aspect of transformation talked about in the book. Your journey may not be as dramatic as what Messiah experienced. But if you're willing to invite God to match your enthusiasm for mission, your "makeover" may lead you to unexpected places, too, just like it did for Messiah. Thanks be!

Chapter 11

The Makeover Tool Chest

When our house experienced main-floor flooding from the record rains that inundated Iowa in 2008, I learned again how having the right tool for the job can make that job so much easier. A nippers was great at pulling nails out of the punky subfloor.

In transformational ministry, two of the best tools to have in one's tool chest are a sense of creativity and a willingness to try things that haven't been done before. In the pages that follow, I offer some ideas, questions, and approaches that have been helpful in makeover ministry settings. These tools are meant to be used in a group setting, ideally with the council, the congregation in various configurations, and the pastor(s) working through them. These tool drawers could also be used as the basis for a series of cottage meetings or as an in-home study group too.

Though anybody can make an assessment of their ministry setting, it's important to bring others on board. One doesn't want to point fingers or lay blame or be a lone ranger trying to get things done. And by all means, if you're reading this on your own, carve out some time to share your thoughts with your pastor(s). Hopefully many of the thoughts and possibilities will serve you well and will serve as springboards for your own thinking, planning, and acting as you seek to do a makeover in your setting.

As with any tool chest, sometimes you have to look around a bit to find the right tool. Sometimes, you also have to improvise in order to do the job. The same thing applies with each of these "tool drawers." They may not be exactly what'll work in your setting, but they can provide a great jumping off spot to get you started. They're also not necessarily designed to be opened consecutively. Assess your ministry setting and see where you'd like to start. All the drawers can be opened, but you don't have to do them all at the same time or even in the same year. A final caveat regarding this tool box and the makeover concept: it is meant to be inspirational — descriptive not proscriptive. What your congregation gets out of this process depends on what you put into it. Blessings!

Drawer 1
Get the Facts

Listening is important in any ministry setting; it may be even more important in a transformational one. People need to tell the story of their congregation, the highs and lows, the successes and setbacks. Certainly, individual conversation is beneficial for learning a congregation's story, but a communal event yields insight, too. Schedule a time when people can gather for meal and guided conversation. We were fortunate at Messiah that shortly after I came, we had the chance for a fortieth anniversary observance. To help learn the congregation's story, we used a process similar to what is offered here. It was great fun!

Create table tents for conversation starters for the meal. Possible questions are listed below. Once you've had your meal, move into large group time, building on the table talk foundation. You know your congregation. If necessary, have more than one meal and conversation time to maximize participation. Maybe you want to schedule the meals over the course of a month. Do what works in your setting.

Table Talk Conversation Starters
  1. What drew you to this congregation?
  2. How have you been involved in this church?
  3. What are a few of your best memories from here?
  4. What else would like to see the congregation do?

Large Group Time. Designate a recorder.
  1. What drew people to your church? Note the diversity of responses.
  2. List the various involvements people have. Study the list to see if some areas are under-represented.
  3. Invite people to share their best memories. Enjoy hearing these feel-good stories! These stories might also help you

assess your congregation's assets and strengths. help with assets, check out *The Great Permissio Asset-Based Field Guide for Congregations,* by copyright 2002, by the Evangelical Lutheran Ch America
4. List all the ideas people have about where they'd like to see their congregation go. Let this be the basis for your strategic plan and to jointly prioritize the ministry and delegate tasks appropriately.

Some congregations may find it helpful to use an outside facilitator to address these issues and/or to get at them. Others may have people in their congregations that do this sort of thing on a regular basis as part of their day job. Again, you know your congregation, so do what's in the best interest of your church, community, and people.

Drawer 2
Keep Moving

In the episode "Dear Sis" on the TV show M*A*S*H, Father Mulcahy wrestles with his frustrations, wondering if his contributions to his unit make a difference. In a letter home to his sister, Mulcahy reveals the peace he finally achieves with his situation when he says, "It doesn't matter whether you feel useful or not when you're moving from one disaster to another. The trick, I guess, is to just keep moving."

It is an instructive quote for transformation. While we don't necessarily move from disaster to disaster, it is important that we maintain momentum, that we keep moving. To help you keep moving, try this process:
1. Start with some vision words or ideas that either describe your community now or where you want to go (such as: welcoming, inclusive, musical, compassionate, supporter of the arts, involved, and so on). What do you want your congregation to be known for? Does it already have a good reputation about certain things that it does? What are those things? List them. When the brainstorming/vision session happens, it may be helpful to tackle one area of your life

together at a time, such as worship, education, outreach, hospitality, finance, property, social justice, or others. Or you can ask the teams at your church responsible for these areas to do their own work as a small group and then come back together for large group conversation.

2. From that vision list, think about how you'd like to build on your strengths. What are some ideas? Make your second list. Short term goals jump-start the process and give you some immediate things to address and some easy access points to involve people. For example, one of things we did in the congregation I currently serve was to take a survey shortly after I came about how we could spiff up the place. We had some specific ideas, and then we set about putting things in place with cleaning out old items, adding a fresh coat of paint to the classrooms, and giving a modest makeover to what became the Fireside Room. From that process came more projects, some which are bigger vision and bigger ticket items, but that's okay. A long-term vision outline allows for the creative flexibility necessary to adapt to changing circumstances while also allowing for some boundaries within which to work for the longer term.

3. From your big idea list, choose three to five achievable goals per area that you can build consensus around. Once you've engaged in this winnowing process, list your short term goals. You may want to select one or two areas to focus on each year. That's your call.

4. Consider what's necessary to meet those goals. List the resources you'll need per goal.

Goal	Resources
Goal	Resources
Goal	Resources
Goal	Resources
Goal	Resources

5. Once the group has agreed on its goals or, if you broke into smaller topical groups, step back to see what the goals have in common. It may be a theme, it may be a direction, it may be vision. From your list of goals, see if you can create a snappy theme for the year that lets the congregation know exactly what the emphasis will be. It may be a year-long emphasis or a seasonal emphasis. What matters is getting a healthy number of people on board, especially those with leadership capacity..

Refer back to your original brainstorming/vision list. Are there some goals/projects that you deferred because you wanted to get something more immediate in place to fire up the congregation? Re-visit some of those bigger projects/ideas/dreams/hopes. Build consensus around two to four of those projects. Evaluate again what the needs are and what the resources are. Begin to craft a vision for the next two to five years, possibly even coming up with a theme for each year that will guide your planning. Continue to publicize your plan and invite people to share their ideas and dreams, also. As new people join your congregation, make sure they're aware of your visioning process and your planning. Post the information, give regular updates, design a handout, put the information on your website, have quarterly meetings — all are possible ways to keep people informed and to help bring in new people too.

Drawer 3
Welcome Children

How does your congregation stack up when it comes to welcoming that much-sought after demographic of families and children? Test yourselves and put a check beside the things you're already doing.

The Basics
1. Are children's bulletins offered weekly?
2. Do children know they're welcome at worship? Do your leaders know the children by name? Are your leaders willing to do high-fives or fist bumps instead of handshakes in the post-worship receiving line?

3. Is there some sort of choir for the children? This can be as basic as the Sunday school students singing in worship regularly. If you're blessed with an abundance of children and choir leadership, how involved in the worship are the choirs? Do they lead liturgy on occasion?
4. Are beginning and more advanced musicians regularly scheduled to share their gifts in worship? Church can be the most encouraging venue for these budding talents to be nurtured.
5. What about children's messages in worship? Do these happen regularly? While they don't have to occur weekly, it's good to have a children's message frequently. Is the pastor willing and able to share leadership of these messages?
6. Are there kid-friendly worship bags with age-appropriate materials visible and available? Encourage families to take turns refilling the bags as a service project option for their confirmands.
7. Are students welcomed at the table either with a blessing or with the meal?
8. Does your congregation have some sort of budget to support youth and family ministry, even if it's only to cover basic supplies?

More Advanced
1. Are families with young children encouraged to sit up front so the kids can see what's going on? In an earlier era, pews way in the back were designated "for families with small children." Is it surprising kids got squirmy?! Let the kids sit up front.
2. Involve children and students in worship in various capacities:
   • invite the confirmation class to write prayers that are then shared during the worship services for a specific number of weeks.
   • ask confirmation mentors and students to share lector duties during Lent or Advent.

- prepare young children to be basket bearers so they can collect the empty communion glasses. Better yet, move toward communion for the very young if you haven't started this process.
- train older youth (high school students) to serve as assisting ministers and communion ministers.
- designate "Student Sundays" where youth can share some worship leadership duties.
- Nominate youth for governing bodies: council, boards, committees (more than just the youth committee, too!).
3. What about creating a "buddy system" that pairs up children with (single) older adults for worship and fellowship? Designate a special Sunday and have the families sit together and then do a simple craft together afterward.
4. What about setting an offering plate in a visible spot and inviting the children to bring their offering up front when the grown-up offering is collected? Host noisy offering Sundays, where kids are encouraged to bring their coins and then those coins are collected in a metal container and "jangled" to the front with the rest of the offering.
5. What about teaching children to give the dismissal by going up front and pronouncing "Go in peace. Serve the Lord," or something similar?

Drawer 4
Pay Attention

Look at your facility. You can either imagine that you're a newcomer or, if you can find someone unfamiliar with your worship space willing to assist you, invite them along and ask them to help scope out your church. Why? Fresh eyes see things regular worshipers often miss. And they can ask great questions, too, about why something is there and what its purpose is. Also, if you have designers or architects or people who keep up with contemporary decorating trends, draft them to help. Harmony of vision and design makes a statement to guests and visitors about the kind of space and place you are.

A Sunday Morning Checklist
Physical Facility

- Are there parking spots available for guests? Or do they have to hike a ways once they've found a place to park?
- Is the entryway warm and inviting? (This can get a little tricky in the winter because of salt buckets and snow shovels, but even so work toward this.)
- Are the bathrooms easy to find? Is there good signage?
- Do you have people posted to welcome folks and direct them as necessary?
- What about the exterior? Does your place look good?

Worship Service

- Are guests welcomed in a gracious way?
- Are newcomers helped to find their way in the service? Are your people trained to assist those who may be unfamiliar with Lutheran liturgy?
- Is an invitation offered for them to consider making your place their worship home?
- Is the bulletin easy to understand? Even in an age of power-point projected worship, the bulletin can still serve a valuable purpose, especially if there are technical difficulties.
- Are your worship leaders comfortable with their tasks? Do they understand the value of making worship flow smoothly and seamlessly?
- Are children incorporated into your worship life?
- Do you allow silences and transition time? For example, do you give people time to prepare for prayer before launching directly into the prayers?
- Does your worship service flow smoothly?
- Are your worship leaders able to roll with the inevitable glitches that can arise despite the best preparations?

Post-worship Time
- Does someone talk with the guests once the service wraps up?
- Do guests know they're welcome to stay? Does someone take responsibility for shepherding them around and helping them make connections with other people?
- What kind of follow-up program do you have in place? Do you contact your guests during the week after they've worshiped with a note of welcome, a gift of cookies or bread, or some other token of appreciation?
- Do you have lay leaders trained to visit with people about your congregation?
- Are there opportunities for the churches in your area to work together? Explore the possibilities for cooperation on Vacation Bible School, holiday gatherings or concerts, summer community worship services, and others. If you do these sorts of cooperative ventures, make sure your worshipers know that. Such shared ministry speaks volumes.

Drawer 5
Share the Ministry

Sharing the ministry is more than simply dividing up the tasks. Sharing the ministry means inviting people to use their talents in ways that build up the community, giving permission to let people try new ideas, creating partnerships between various groups and individuals, and being willing to realize that the pastor is dispensable. Life can get so much easier for pastors when we realize that we are not always necessary.

Try your hand at evaluating your congregation's openness to sharing the ministry of your church. With 1 indicating "not receptive" and 7 being "very receptive," circle the number that represents where you see your congregation in relation to the items listed below.

1) Create opportunities for new members to get involved sooner rather than later

1   2   3   4
            5   6   7

2) Train and invite lay people to do tasks previously associated with the pastor (such as taking holy communion to shut-ins, preaching, and so on)

1	2	3	4
	5	6	7

3) Have the freedom to test-drive new ideas without having to go through a lot of "proper channels"

1	2	3	4
	5	6	7

4) Wish pastor/council/administration would offer more opportunities for lay people to share their time and talents

1	2	3	4
	5	6	7

5) Expect the pastor to do most of the ministry and mission of the church

1	2	3	4
	5	6	7

Take a look at where your answers line up. Are you all over the grid? What do the numbers tell you? Do you see any sort of pattern?

Shift to Short Answers
(These questions can be applied to a host of ideas simply by varying the answer to the first question.)
- Something I would really like to see happen is:
- I am willing to do this to help bring my idea to life:
- What will be gained if this idea goes forward?
- What ideas in the congregation might need to shift/change in order for this to happen?
- What might we/the congregation/the staff have to give-up or let go of if this idea goes forward? Is that a risk people are willing to take?
- I can help educate people about why this change/ possibility matters by doing the following things and taking the following steps:

FOR PASTORS: Do you have a pastor-parish relationship team? People whom you can confide in about the overall status of the congregation's ministry and people who will be truth tellers that you can listen to without being offended? If so, do the previous section with them if you feel "stuck" trying to move things forward.

Drawer 6
Communicate Clearly

Keeping in mind that the nature of how people communicate has changed drastically with the advent of social media, this tool kit asks you to take an honest and critical look at your primary modes of communication. Consult outside experts if they're available — a journalism teacher, a writer, editor, or someone familiar with layout and design.

Bulletin (if you still use one):
- Does it facilitate the flow of worship?
- Is there a minimum of distraction?
- Is there too much text and not enough white space?

Screens and projectors:
- Does your projection equipment enhance or detract from your worship space?
- Is your service easy to follow?
- Can various media be used interchangeably and handily if the speaker wants to project something?

Newsletter
- How's your layout?
- Are you consistent with what goes where each month?
- What about your typefaces? Are they easy to read?
- Are your pictures big enough? Do you identify what's going on?
- Is your news current?
- Does your format— weekly, semi-monthly or monthly — meet the needs of your parish?
- Is your newsletter available online?

- Do you proofread your newsletter even after you've used the spelling and grammar checks?

Website
- Is your website eye-catching and easy to navigate?
- Is your news up to date?
- Do you post the changes in worship time there, too?
- Is your content relevant without being overwhelming?

Social Media Presence

As mentioned in the corresponding chapter, social media is a growing edge for this pastor. However, there are ways to use it that I have come to appreciate. Using it wisely and well in the parish will be important, so I offer these ideas:

Get a copy of Meredith Gould's book The Social Media Gospel. Read it alone and/or with your staff. It's a thorough, helpful read and gives the reader a great overview of the different kinds of media and how each can be most useful. She also makes valid points about how different learning styles work in tandem with the various media that congregations use to reach their people.

Since kids are almost always ahead of their parents on using newer technologies, are you helping your parents and families find their way through the array of sites out there?

Are you or someone on your staff on Twitter, Tumblr, Instagram, Vine, or whatever else is current by the time this book is published to keep in touch with your youth? Are you using these to keep tabs on what they are doing and being the "community watchdog" so you or your staff have a sense of when the students might need a little extra guidance or help?

Is your message on social media consistent with what you preach and teach? Are you the same gracious presence in your posts and feeds that you try to be in the parish? Along with that, does social media accurately reflect your congregation?

Drawer 7
Learn Your Lessons
Part 1: Stewardship

Pastor: If you were to grade the congregation's overall stewardship (regular offerings, special collections, materials shared such as quilts and kits and so on) what would you give them? Why?

Leadership Team Members: If you were to grade the congregation's overall stewardship (regular offerings, special collections, materials shared such as quilts and kits, and so forth) what would you give them? Why?
- Discuss your answers and insights. Is there room to grow both in understanding of stewardship and of giving?
- What kinds of stewardship education has the congregation done? Who has been in charge of heading that up?
- Do you wish you had a year-round stewardship education program? How about the question of financial or spiritual issues related to giving?
- Take a look at your mission investment goals/budget. What does it say about where you're investing yourselves? Does this reflect how you see yourselves and your strengths?

In what areas would you like to grow your giving? What will you need to do in order to get there? Consider doing a SWOT analysis as you ponder the next steps: Strengths, weaknesses, opportunities, threats (or tangles or tripper-uppers, if you prefer. I don't particularly like that word "threats," so feel free to think differently here.)

Part 2: Dealing with Tough Stuff
- What struggles has the congregation experienced?
- How can the congregation's history be helpful in terms of working through current tough issues? Being familiar with the congregational history, either through reading or talking with the "seasoned saints" of the church is a valuable tool in finding one's way through tricky spots.

If they have a history, for example, of having faithfully addressed difficult issues without fracturing, how can that be helpful now as part of the congregation's identity?
- How do you address difficult issues?
- What are some valuable lessons you've already learned?
- What are you willing to risk for? What are you willing to let go of for the sake of the health and good order of the congregation?
- Do you have a clearly stated policy of how people in the body of Christ will communicate and interact with one another? If not, are you willing to craft a statement on how people in the body of Christ will interact with each other if things get heated?

Drawer 8
Mine Your Assets

A few key passages guided the transformation at Janesville. The chapter mentioned Jeremiah 29:11 and 2 Corinthians 5: 17. Also significant was 2 Timothy 1:7. What scripture passages undergird and support your ministry? Are there a few key pegs on which your ministry depends? What are they? Does the congregation know them?

Using the 6 steps outlined from the "Mia Makeover" scene mentioned in The Princess Diaries, begin the work. If you can access a copy of the movie, watch the makeover scene with your group in conjunction with this discussion.

1. Take a closer look at your congregation.
- List the scripture stories and passages at the heart of your ministry:
- Why are these passages significant? What do they say about you as a congregation?
- Are there other passages that speak about your life together as a congregation? What are they? Why are they meaningful?
- What's beautiful about your place? Architecture, people, spirit, attitudes? Even if there's heartache or pain, there are still beautiful things to be found. What are they? List them.

- Take a strength inventory of your people and your place.
- What resources does your congregation have? Your community? What resources do they need? Where do your resources and the community's needs intersect?

2. Let the work begin.

Are people ready to get involved? Are they ready to roll up their sleeves for transformation? Do they have the information they need to proceed? Are there projects for people to help with? Is the pastor willing to share the workload?
- What projects are going well?
- What tasks need attention?
- Who does these things?
- Who else can you ask to get involved?

3. Have the right tools

What tools do you need to communicate your ministry? Do you need to walk the neighborhoods? Do you need to put ads in the paper or increase your social media presence? Do you need to be a community resource? Do those who don't believe in your ministry need to hear the good news stories regularly and from a variety of sources and then be encouraged to be more supportive and less vocal in their dislikes?
- What tools work well in your ministry setting? List them.
- Are there other things you'd like to do or try? What are they? List them.

4. Beware of distractions

With a makeup kit, it can be easy to accumulate a lot of products that don't really suit your style. Those items can also get in the way of finding what you really need for your makeover. The same kind of thing can happen in a ministry setting. We can get all caught up in lots of things that take the focus away from transformation, especially when it seems like there are numerous tasks to accomplish. Stop a minute. Breathe. Pray. Think.

- Consider what is essential to your ministry. List those things.
- Think about when you get distracted or sidetracked. How does that happen? What things do you need to watch out for? List them.
- How can you minimize those distractions? What's your plan? Can you delegate? Can you ask for help? Jot down some ideas. Who are some people you're comfortable sharing the plan with for accountability's sake?

5. Break things.

I do not mean physically, of course, unless it's ground for a new building project. That's exciting! Sometimes, old patterns need to be examined, tweaked, or altogether given up in order for new life to arise. One specific thing we did was to get away from the idea that only the women of the church (altar guild) could get the worship space ready. We opened this venture up to families and ended up having "worship prep teams" instead. It made for some good intergenerational ministry.

- Are there some less than healthy behaviors in your congregation? What might some of those things be?
- What are some ideas for addressing those behaviors?
- How critical is each behavior? Prioritize what needs to be addressed now and what can wait until later. Do you need to bring in outside help to deal with the situation?

6. Get outside help.

This particular part of the tool drawer is designed especially for pastors and leads into the next chapters, also.

In this section, you'll put together a list of go to people who can serve as resources for you and your ministry. Here's an overview of why that's necessary:

1. "Outside help" can mean any number of things, and sometimes the help is available in your community just by talking with people who've been in the area a long time, with people who know the trends and traditions

of your area. Talking with people such as the chief of police, the school principal(s) or superintendent, medical professionals, prominent business leaders and "community pillars" is a smart move.
2. Beyond conversation and community bridge building, those interactions say to your parish that you really are interested in the community and in finding out how your church can serve as a resource. Don't underestimate how valuable your visibility can be! Other resources can include workshops, seminars, books, and periodicals relative to what you're dealing with and/or trying to accomplish.
3. In all of this, partner with your judicatory and its staff. Keep them in the loop about what you're doing, what you're hearing and what reactions you're receiving. My interactions with the synod staff made me aware of strategies, workshops and others in the area who were working on similar projects, and I found people eager and willing to help effect transformation. Your judicatory may also be able to make connections on your behalf with other congregations.
4. Since many pastors still tend toward the "Lone Ranger" model of ministry, keep in mind that one's colleagues can also be great resources. Attending small and large group conferences and colleague meetings gives you the chance to refresh and renew, and I often gleaned ideas from colleague and conference meetings. Besides that, the time away is good "thinking time" and gives you an opportunity to reflect that might not ordinarily happen in the midst of hectic days of transformation mission and ministry.

My Go-to-People

Take a few minutes and jot down the names of people that you've turned to already in your ministry for ideas, support, truth-telling, and encouragement.
- Think about your community. Who are some other people that might be good to visit with? What qualities do they have that make you want to visit with them?

- What about outside your immediate area?
- What about books or periodicals that might be helpful? Do you already own them? Are you already a subscriber? Is your congregation aware of these resources too?
- Has there been a situation in the past year or two where you involved your judicatory? How did that go? Evaluate how your interaction went to see what you've learned.
- Has there been a situation in the past year or two where you wished you would have involved your judicatory? What got in the way of asking for help or being in conversation? How will you handle things differently if there is a "next time?"

Drawers 9 and 10
Looking to the Future and Leaving Well

Sometimes, tool chests have really big drawers to accommodate larger tools. This particular section is designed with that image in mind. Looking to the future and leaving well involve evaluating options and possibilities, as well as a candid assessment of one's ministry.

To leave wisely and well is often a challenge in ministry. If we have loved the people and let them love us, saying goodbye is hard. If things have not gone well, that presents its own difficulties, too. Let's look at some things we can do to help the leave-taking process.

1. Do some honest reflection on your ministry: Have you accomplished the majority of what you were called to do?

List some of those accomplishments.

2. Are there new projects and possibilities in the parish that still excite you?

List some of those possibilities.

3. How's your family doing in the currrent ministry setting?

4. Are there good reasons for your family to stay in the current setting? List them.

5. Are there good reasons for your family to leave the current setting? List them.

6. What about a sabbatical? Is this something you'd like to work toward? How much lead time do you need to plan? It may take over a year to get ready. Who needs to be in on the sabbatical planning process? What would you hope to gain in your current setting if you pursued a sabbatical?

7. How are your finances? Have you analyzed your situation? Would you be able to make it until another call came along? Or are you stuck? If you're stuck, what do you need to make it through this time, to be refreshed and renewed, if that's possible? Have you talked to anyone about your situation? Depending on how you answer those questions, you may or may not need to have a sit-down with your judicatory to talk about options for your future.

8. After going through the assessment offered in this chapter, and with plenty of prayer and reflection, size up your ministry. What does your head tell you? What does your heart tell you?
   • If you're feeling called to stay where you are, what are some plans for staying?
   • If you're feeling called to move on, what items need to be addressed? How do you want the congregation to honor your ministry and thank you (and your family, if applicable) for serving them? It's important that congregations be given a chance to say thank you. It's important for pastors to be given the same opportunity, as well as the chance to offer and receive forgiveness for those missteps along the way.

For Clergy

Take some time for self-reflection in this section.
- What have been some of the best moments in your ministry? How did those come about?

- If you were to define your pastoral style with one word, what word would you choose?

- Would others agree with you? Why or why not?

- Are there some things about your pastoral style that you've given some thought to changing?

- Think back to some things that didn't go so well; what happened there? Why?

- Do you have a colleague or two you trust and can turn to? Are you willing to ask them for a candid assessment of your strengths and areas of concern?

Afterword

Well, there you have it, kind reader, a story of renewal and hope in a particular place and a particular time, with a few other stories, snippets and insights from my years in ministry. Thank you for going along with me.

In the 27-plus years since I interned as a student pastor and then entered the ministry, I've served in small, mid-sized and larger parishes in Iowa. I've been in my current call at St. Timothy in Hudson since 2011. Together, we effected renewal through a major facility renovation in 2018-2019 and also through a time of necessary healing following a rough and divisive patch in 2009-2010. It hasn't always been easy, and I've made my share of mistakes along the way, but what I've learned since leaving Janesville and from the other congregations open to renewal is that it's important for congregations to keep moving.

Similar to the importance of keeping our bodies in motion as we age, congregations benefit when they're willing to try new things—willing to move forward in faith. Some things may flop. That's okay. Try something else. Some things may stick. Enjoy those successes!

This book is more descriptive than proscriptive. I hope that after reading these stories, you're inspired to find ways in your context that you can be ever more open to God's renewing spirit. Whether you wade gently into the shallow end of the renewal pool or dive enthusiastically into the deep end, I pray that you'll be able to celebrate your own stories of hope, renewal and possibility.

About the Author

When Pastor Beth Olson and her family accepted the call to serve in Janesville, Iowa, a small town in the heartland, the future of the struggling congregation was unsure. The members had known economic upset, pastorates that hadn't quite clicked, and uncertainties about what kind of future awaited them.

But over the course of more than nine years together, and with the right combination of hope, persistence, and enthusiasm for the mission God called them to, the congregation and the pastor experienced a transformation — a makeover — that provided new possibilities in ways the congregation couldn't have dreamed of when they made the decision to move forward in faith and mission for the sake of the gospel.

Olson has previously shared her congregation's makeover story in events sponsored by the ELCA's Division for Outreach, the Northeastern Iowa Synod Assembly, and at various informal gatherings. She has served as a conference dean, an internship supervisor, a conference chaplain, and is currently serving as a member of her judicatory's First Call Theological Education committee.

Additionally, her articles about including children in worship have appeared in the Augsburg Fortress worship resource book Sundays and Seasons 2009. She has written prayers (2007, 2008, 2009) for Bread for the Day, a daily devotional book also published by Augsburg Fortress, and her poetry has been published in the 64th edition of Lyrical Iowa. She and her family live in Waverly, Iowa. This is her first book.

CPSIA information can be obtained
at www.ICGtesting.com
Printed in the USA
FSHW011151270619
59434FS